DRIVEN TO MURDER

by Olive Chase
and Stanley Clayton

Copyright © 1978 by Olive Chase and Stanley Clayton
All Rights Reserved

DRIVEN TO MURDER is fully protected under the copyright laws of the British Commonwealth, including Canada, the United States of America, and all other countries of the Copyright Union. All rights, including professional and amateur stage productions, recitation, lecturing, public reading, motion picture, radio broadcasting, television, online/digital production, and the rights of translation into foreign languages are strictly reserved.

ISBN 978-0-573-11107-5

concordtheatricals.co.uk
concordtheatricals.com

FOR PRODUCTION ENQUIRIES

UNITED KINGDOM AND WORLD
EXCLUDING NORTH AMERICA
licensing@concordtheatricals.co.uk
020-7054-7200

Each title is subject to availability from Concord Theatricals, depending upon country of performance.

CAUTION: Professional and amateur producers are hereby warned that *DRIVEN TO MURDER* is subject to a licensing fee. The purchase, renting, lending or use of this book does not constitute a licence to perform this title(s), which licence must be obtained from the appropriate agent prior to any performance. Performance of this title(s) without a licence is a violation of copyright law and may subject the producer and/or presenter of such performances to penalties. Both amateurs and professionals considering a production are strongly advised to apply to the appropriate agent before starting rehearsals, advertising, or booking a theatre. A licensing fee must be paid whether the title is presented for charity or gain and whether or not admission is charged.

This work is published by Samuel French, an imprint of Concord Theatricals Ltd.

No one shall make any changes in this title for the purpose of production. No part of this book may be reproduced, stored in a retrieval system, scanned, uploaded, or transmitted in any form, by any means, now known or yet to be invented, including mechanical, electronic, digital, photocopying, recording, videotaping, or otherwise, without the prior written permission of the publisher. No one shall share this title, or part of this title, to any social media or file hosting websites.

The moral right of Olive Chase and Stanley Clayton to be identified as author of this work has been asserted in accordance with Section 77 of the Copyright, Designs and Patents Act 1988.

USE OF COPYRIGHTED MUSIC

A licence issued by Concord Theatricals to perform this play does not include permission to use the incidental music specified in this publication. In the United Kingdom: Where the place of performance is already licensed by the PERFORMING RIGHT SOCIETY (PRS) a return of the music used must be made to them. If the place of performance is not so licensed then application should be made to PRS for Music (www.prsformusic.com). A separate and additional licence from PHONOGRAPHIC PERFORMANCE LTD. (www.ppluk.com) may be needed whenever commercial recordings are used. Outside the United Kingdom: Please contact the appropriate music licensing authority in your territory for the rights to any incidental music.

USE OF COPYRIGHTED THIRD-PARTY MATERIALS

Licensees are solely responsible for obtaining formal written permission from copyright owners to use copyrighted third-party materials (e.g., artworks, logos) in the performance of this play and are strongly cautioned to do so. If no such permission is obtained by the licensee, then the licensee must use only original materials that the licensee owns and controls. Licensees are solely responsible and liable for clearances of all third-party copyrighted materials, and shall indemnify the copyright owners of the play(s) and their licensing agent, Concord Theatricals Ltd., against any costs, expenses, losses and liabilities arising from the use of such copyrighted third-party materials by licensees.

IMPORTANT BILLING AND CREDIT REQUIREMENTS

If you have obtained performance rights to this title, please refer to your licensing agreement for important billing and credit requirements.

CHARACTERS

John Ferryman

Dr Helen Ferryman, his wife

Susan Lovat, Dr Ferryman's daughter

Michael Eastwood

Mrs Parks

Mary Eastwood

Detective Chief Inspector Ian Conway

Mr Watson

Rita Davies

Policewoman Baker (optional character*)

The action takes place in the main room of the Ferrymans' bungalow at 102 Parkside Avenue and in a corner of a room at 37 Parkside Avenue

ACT I The Ferrymans' bungalow. A spring evening. 8 p.m.

ACT II SCENE 1 No. 37 Parkside Avenue. The same evening. 8.45 p.m.
SCENE 2 The Ferrymans' bungalow. The following morning. 9.30 a.m.

ACT III SCENE 1 The Ferrymans' bungalow. The same morning. 10.30 a.m.
SCENE 2 The same, about 11.30 a.m.

Alternatively, the play can be staged in two acts with the interval after ACT II, SCENE 1

Time—the present

* If desired Policewoman Baker need not appear. Only slight alterations to the text are required.

ACT I

The open-plan lounge/dining-room of the Ferrymans' bungalow. An evening in Spring

The overall impression should be that of a modern, recently furnished and decorated, but well-used house. Everything is in very good taste. On the right of the stage a door leads to the hall and the rest of the bungalow. Below it is an electric fire and shelf fitment holding a television, radio, etc. On the other side of the stage is a door leading to the kitchen, rear entrance and garage. At the back is a window overlooking the front garden. To the left of the window is a room divider, about five feet high, separating the dining area which is raised by a single step and holds a dining-table, chairs and small sideboard. There is a hatch to the kitchen. The furniture in the lounge consists of a settee with a coffee table in front of it and a sofa table behind it. There is a low armchair below the fire and a small table with a telephone on it above the kitchen door. In front of the window is a trough containing plants

When the CURTAIN *rises it is almost dark outside the room, although the curtains are not drawn. The lights are on and the fire glows. John Ferryman is sitting at the dining-table engrossed in some papers. He is in his early forties, a seemingly quiet, pleasant and considerate man, apparently lacking in decision at times but really shrewd and persistent. Dr Helen Ferryman enters from the kitchen carrying a tray of coffee things. She is in her late thirties, attractive, outwardly composed, strong-minded yet with warmth and emotion. She crosses and puts the tray down on the coffee table*

Helen Coffee's ready, John
John (*gathering his papers*) Right!
Helen (*going to the hall door and calling*) Coffee, Susan.

Helen starts to pour coffee. The telephone rings and John answers it

John (*on the telephone*) Orrell two-two-one-five. . . . Dr Ferryman? Just a minute. (*To Helen*) It's for you. A patient.
Helen I was half expecting it.

Helen takes the receiver. John goes to the settee

Helen (*on the telephone*) Yes? . . . When did you give him the last dose? . . . Give him another one now and if there's no reaction in half an hour let me know. . . . That's right. . . . Good-bye. (*She replaces the receiver and returns to the settee*)
John (*fussing over her, moving cushions, etc.*) I though it was your night off. (*He passes her coffee*)

Helen (*smiling her thanks*) It's supposed to be, but I warned you before we were married that a doctor is never really off duty. (*She indicates his folder*) I'm beginning to think accountants are the same. Another late night?

John I'm afraid so

Helen That's the fourth this week.

John And the last. I have to finish the scheme and let Mr Martin have it before half past eleven tomorrow. That's when he leaves for New York. Look, why don't you give it up?

Helen Um?

John Doctoring. You don't *have* to do it you know. Thanks to you I can keep us going.

Helen I know that. It isn't the money. It's—well I think doctors are born—not made, and if you're born that way, to stop would be a waste. Or am I being swollen headed?

John I don't think so.

Helen It *is* only part time. And as long as we have Mrs Parks . . .

John (*disgustedly*) Mrs Parks!

Helen I know. She doesn't know her place. She's the biggest gossip in the district. But she's willing and she keeps the place spotless.

John Clinical is the word

Helen If you only knew how difficult it is to get *anybody* . . .

John I'll say no more. Where's Susan? The coffee will be getting cold.

Helen Glamourising I imagine. She had a shopping spree this afternoon and she's going to a dance tonight with Michael.

John Again? She's seeing a lot of him these days. Is it serious?

Helen At seventeen?

John Seventeen's grown up. At least seventeen thinks so.

Helen Would you mind—if Susan were serious?

John (*rather bitterly*) Would it make the slightest difference if I did?

Helen John!

John (*putting his cup down and rising*) Well, let's face it, dear. We've been married a year and things haven't changed a bit. Susan resents me as much now as she did when we first told her, and you know what a scene there was then.

Helen She said a lot of things she didn't mean.

John The word was fortune-hunter—and I think she meant it.

Helen Is that why you want me to give up the practice?

John I doubt if that would stop her reminding me whose money bought me a partnership in the firm. I'm sorry, dear. (*He sits down again*) If she wants to get engaged to Michael and it makes you happy—I'll give them my blessing. He's about the steadiest boy she's brought home so far.

Helen I'm not sure that Susan would consider that a compliment. But from what I hear about his mother I gather it's a miracle. Of all the possessive, neurotic women. Still, I suppose there's some excuse. I understand she had a bad time when her husband died.

John (*putting his arm round her and drawing her to him*) So had you. But you came through all right. (*He sniffs her hair appreciatively*) You smell very nice tonight. What is it?

Act I 3

Helen You should know. You gave it to me for Christmas.
John I always did have good taste. (*He kisses her*)

Susan enters from the hall and reacts to what she sees. She is a pretty girl with definite ideas and all the over-confidence of one so young. She is dressed in an up-to-the-minute outfit including a pair of distinctive earrings. John senses her presence and breaks away

Susan (*posing in the doorway*) Do you like it?
Helen (*rather taken aback she looks at Susan then glances at John, then back to Susan*) Well—it's—it's very smart, dear. But isn't it just—a little bit . . .
Susan (*coming into the room*) I'm going to a disco at the Rugby Club—not the Mayor's Ball.
Helen I appreciate that. But don't you think that people might get the wrong idea?
Susan Oh, Mother!
Helen What do you think, John?
John (*standing up and moving towards Susan*) Turn round.

John tries to put his hand on Susan's shoulder but Susan deliberately moves away

(*Quietly*) It's—it's very nice.
Susan I suppose *you'd* prefer sackcloth and ashes.
Helen Susan!
John (*quietly*) It doesn't matter, Helen. (*He moves back to the coffee table and picks up the folder*) Susan's going out with Michael not with us. (*He goes to the door and turns to Susan*) I'll be working late in the study so don't worry about locking up. I'll see to it. And don't disturb your mother when you come in. She needs an early night. Have a good time.

John exits

Helen (*rising and facing Susan*) You'll go this minute and apologize to John.
Susan He has no right to criticize.
Helen He *is* your stepfather.
Susan He's John Ferryman—and I'm Susan Lovat.
Helen Why do you dislike him so much?
Susan Because he's a phoney. Because he's too polite and patient—and milk-and-watery—and I hate him.
Helen How dare you!
Susan You can't have it both ways, Mother. Either you want to know what I think of my stepfather, or you don't. If you don't, say so, and I'll keep quiet, but if you do—then you've got to let me tell it my way.
Helen (*after a moment*) Go on.
Susan When my father died things weren't easy for you. You hadn't a practice. You were just a widow with a child to bring up. There were no

men begging you to marry them—but as soon as those shares my father left you turned into a small fortune there was Mr John Ferryman knocking on the door. The answer to a lonely widow's prayer.

Helen John knew nothing about the money.

Susan That's what *he* says. *I* think he was waiting until he knew you were able to buy him a permanent meal ticket.

Helen Then why is he still working?

Susan And how long do you think that's going to last now you've bought him a nice, fat partnership?

Helen John's going to pay me back.

Susan I'll bet.

Helen All right! All right! Suppose the money *did* make a difference. Suppose John *does* stop working. I tell you it isn't important.

Susan (*flinging herself into the armchair*) Oh, mother!

Helen You never really knew the father you idolized.

Susan That's not true.

Helen He was nothing like the picture you've built up in your mind.

Susan (*putting her hands over her ears*) I don't want to hear.

Helen (*pulling her hands away*) You wanted to have this out and you're going to listen until I've finished. (*Quieter*) You only remember the pleasant things about Simon, you've forgotten that he never earned a penny in his life. That all he left behind were debts. That he used the shares you talk about to swindle two old people out of their life savings.

Susan And I suppose he was to blame for the way he died!

Helen If he hadn't been driving too fast to get away from the police he wouldn't have crashed the car and it wouldn't have caught fire.

Susan (*vehemently*) It's lies—all lies! You're just making excuses for getting married again.

Helen I don't need excuses—I married John because I loved him. He wasn't the first man who asked me—but I was afraid you'd hate me if I put someone in Simon's place.

Susan And what had John Ferryman to offer to make the risk worthwhile?

Helen Things that Simon never gave me. Thoughtfulness—honesty—trust. Besides I'd realized you would never change and I wanted someone to think of me instead of me having to think of other people. I needed companionship—love. I wanted a man about the house again.

Susan (*viciously*) Even If you had to buy one?

Susan rises and they stand face to face, Helen with her hand raised as if to strike Susan

Suddenly Susan swings on her heels and exits through the hall. After a pause there is a knock on the kitchen door which Helen disregards. After a moment Michael Eastwood enters. He is a pleasant, intelligent, rather reserved man of about twenty. Most mothers would be pleased to have him as a son-in-law. His dress is up-to-date but not extreme. At the moment he is tense, obviously with something on his mind. He has a cold. With him he has a small suitcase which he leaves by the kitchen door

Act I

Michael Oh, Mrs Ferryman. I knocked but no-one seemed to hear.
Helen I—I was just coming. But I'm afraid Susan isn't ready yet.
Michael That's all right. I—I wanted to see Mr Ferryman first.
Helen Is something wrong? Something to do with Susan?
Michael Yes.
Helen Well, I'm her mother.
Michael I'm sorry. I'd rather talk to Mr Ferryman. Please—it's important.
Helen (*after a moment*) I'll call him. (*She goes to the hall door and calls*) John—will you come here a minute?

As Helen moves back into the room Michael sneezes

Helen You seem to have a cold.
Michael I woke with it this morning. Mother talked me into taking some kind of cold cure tablets. They seem to be doing the trick though my head is still a bit muzzy.

John enters from the hall

John Oh, good evening, Michael, I didn't hear you arrive.
Michael Could I speak to you alone.
John (*hesitating and looking at Helen*) Well . . . I . . .
Helen If it concerns Susan I'm staying.
John You might as well go ahead Michael.
Michael (*acutely uncomfortable but realizing Helen is quite determined to stay*) A—a little while ago I had a phone call. It—it accused Susan and me of going further than we should.
Helen What!
John (*quietly*) Helen. (*To Michael*) By going further—you mean going to bed together?
Michael Yes.
John An anonymous call of course.
Michael Yes.
John Man or woman?
Michael A man.
John There's no truth in what he said?
Michael (*strongly*) Of course not!
John Then why are you so scandalized? After all, it's not unknown for a certain type of crank to make calls like that.
Michael There was something else. He said there were photographs— and afterwards—this was pushed through the letter-box.

Michael hands an envelope to John. As John takes a photograph out of it Helen tries to look at it

Michael Mrs Ferryman. I don't think you should . . .
John (*moving so that Helen cannot see*) Just a minute, dear. (*He looks at the photograph, grim-faced*) I know what you mean Michael—but I think Helen should see it.

John hands the photograph to Helen whose face registers horror and disgust. She sinks on to the settee

Helen No! No! This isn't Susan.
Michael It isn't me, either.
Helen I didn't mean that. But the faces. Yours—and Susan's ...
John ... could easily be superimposed by anyone who knows anything about photography. (*To Michael*) You swear there's nothing ...
Michael I've already told you.
John Has anyone else seen this?
Michael My mother may have done. She overheard the phone call—and found the envelope first.
John Did she say anything?
Michael Doesn't she always? The trouble is she never listens. I said it was a leg pull—but she went on and on about me wasting time with Susan instead of studying. It's the same old record—time and time again—so I walked out to avoid a row.
Helen This time perhaps it's just as well. Why should someone do anything as vicious as this?
John Was there any demand for money?
Michael No.
John Then it's not blackmail. (*He tries to take the photograph from Helen*) Looking at it won't do any good.
Helen (*refusing to let go*) Just a minute. Those ear-rings. Aren't they the ones we gave Susan for her birthday?
John (*taking and studying the photograph*) Yes—yes they are.
Helen That's only three weeks ago. (*To Michael*) Aren't there photographers at those dos you go to?
Michael Only from the local papers.
John What about the ones who wander about with flash-guns?
Michael I wouldn't know.
John Wouldn't the organizers?
Michael I doubt it. And I'd rather not ask the police.
Helen (*firmly*) We're not going to the organizers—or the police.
John But Helen ...
Helen It might—just—be—be a horrible, sick joke.
Michael (*incredulously*) A joke!
Helen Do you want to show that photograph to anyone?
Michael Of course not! But hadn't you better see what Susan says. Someone has to tell her.
Helen Yes—yes, of course. I'll do it. (*Holding out her hand to John*) Let me have—that.

John gives her the photograph and puts an arm round her shoulders

John Would you like me to stay?
Helen No. I'd rather talk to her on my own.
John All right. I'll call her. Come on, Michael, we'll wait in the study.

Act I 7

John and Michael exit to the hall

(*Off*) Susan, your mother wants you.

A moment later Susan enters wearing a coat and carrying a week-end case. She closes the door and leans against it

Helen (*staring at the case*) Where are you going with that?
Susan (*puzzled*) To the dance. I told you this afternoon. It's in aid of Oxfam. Everyone has to take some used clothing.
Helen I'd forgotten.
Susan Did you think I was running away?
Helen I never know what you'll do when your in one of your moods.
Susan Well one thing I'm not going to do is apologize for what I said about my stepfather—because I think it's true. (*She puts the case down and goes to Helen*) But I'll apologize for what I said about you. I'm sorry, Mother—I—I just blew my top.
Helen (*holding her for a moment*) Thank you. But that's not what I wanted you for. Come and sit down.
Susan I haven't much time. Michael's due any minute.
Helen Michael's here now.
Susan Here? Where?
Helen In the study with John.
Susan What's he doing there?
Helen If you sit down I'll tell you.

Puzzled, Susan sits on the settee. Helen stands behind her

Just before Michael left home—he had an anonymous phone call—and this—came—

Helen pushes the photograph into Susan's hand. Susan looks at her baffled then looks at the photograph. She stiffens but shows no other reaction

Susan (*after a moment*) Wow! Poor old Michael.
Helen (*Astounded*) What!
Susan Well he is a bit straight-laced.
Helen Is that all you have to say?
Susan What do you want me to say? Do you believe this shows either of us?
Helen Of course not.
Susan Then what?
Helen There *are* other people.
Susan Is Michael going to show it to them? Are you?
Helen There could be other copies.
Susan Then we'll deal with them when we find them.
Helen I don't understand you.
Susan You thought I'd have hysterics. Well—later—maybe I will. When it really hits me—maybe I'll get drunk or cry myself to sleep. But right now I just feel sorry.

Helen Sorry!

Susan For someone out there—with a sick mind. Do you want this? (*She holds out the photograph*)

Helen shakes her head. Susan rises, tears the photograph up and drops the pieces into the waste-paper basket

Hadn't you better let them come back?

Helen (*still only half comprehending, opens the door and calls*) Michael!

Michael enters and goes straight to Susan

Michael If—if you'd rather not go to the dance—it's all right. I don't mind.

Susan Why shouldn't I want to go?

Michael I . . . I don't know—I thought—perhaps . . .

Susan You thought someone might ask us if we'd had any good photographs taken lately.

Helen Susan!

Susan (*quickly and firmly*) This is between Michael and me. Well, Michael?

Michael If I ever find out who did it I'll beat the living daylights out of him.

He holds out his hand to Susan, who takes it

Susan Damn him! That's what I say. We're not going to let him spoil our fun. Shall we go?

Helen No, wait, Susan. When did you have your photograph taken wearing those ear-rings?

John enters R. He remains in the doorway

Susan (*instinctively feeling the ear-rings*) These? I don't know. (*Suddenly remembering*) Yes I do. Last week at the Press Ball. The man with the black beard.

Michael I—I don't remember.

Susan I was coming from the powder-room. There was a flash and I saw this man walking away.

Helen Would you recognize him again?

Susan No.

Michael Is that the only time you can remember?

Susan No! No, it isn't. (*She goes to John*) At my birthday party—when you gave me the ear-rings—you took some snap-shots and developed the films yourself.

John opens his mouth to retaliate—but says nothing

Helen Oh, Susan!

Helen turns away angrily towards the window. She stops suddenly as she sees a bearded face with dark glasses—Mr Watson—peering in. Their eyes meet

Act I

for a moment and then the man hurries away. Helen gasps with shock and recognition. As she turns into the room there is a muffled scream from the garden

John (*to Michael, indicating the kitchen door*) You go that way!

Michael goes towards the kitchen door as John makes for the hall door. Helen tries to block his way

Helen No John. Wait!

As Michael reaches the door Mrs Parks bursts in. She is agitated, out of breath, and slightly dishevelled. She is a hard-working, out-spoken busybody of indeterminate age, with a slight working-class accent

John Mrs Parks!
Mrs Parks Attacked! That's what I've been. Attacked by a man in the garden!
John After him, Michael.

Michael exits

Susan takes Mrs Parks' arm and helps her to a chair. John moves towards the hall door

Helen No, John! You might get hurt. In any case it's no use going that way.
John Why not?
Helen If he'd crossed the garden I would have seen him through the window. And I didn't. I didn't see anyone.
John Steady, dear, steady.
Helen He's probably climbed over into the park. If you must go out go with Michael. Then there'll be two of you to deal with him.
John All right. And if you're getting Mrs Parks a drink I think you'd better have one yourself.

John exits through the kitchen

Helen (*to Mrs Parks*) Are you hurt?
Mrs Parks Well—nothing broken.

Helen goes to the sideboard and pours out drinks

Susan (*taking Mrs Parks' hat off*) Lets get rid of this.
Mrs Parks Ruined—that's what it is.
Susan Well, knocked about a bit.
Mrs Parks Same as me dear.
Susan And just look at your coat. (*She brushes Mrs Parks down*) Do you feel like telling us what happened?
Mrs Parks Coming round the back I was, dear—when I see this face staring at me—big dark glasses and a beard—and before I could move...

Susan Did you say a beard?

Mrs Parks A real door mat. Now like I was saying, before I could move...

Helen (*handing a glass to Mrs Parks*) You'd better drink this.

Mrs Parks (*suspiciously*) What is it?

Helen Brandy. Purely medicinal.

Mrs Parks Oh, well that's different, isn't it. (*She downs the drink in one gulp, pulling a face and shuddering*) Not that I wouldn't rather have a nice hot cup of tea.

Helen Are you sure nothing's damaged?

Mrs Parks Only me dignity—and you ain't got no pills for that.

Helen Then you stay here and I'll put the kettle on. Draw the curtains will you, Susan?

Helen exits to the kitchen

Susan Did you recognize him?
Mrs Parks Eh!
Susan The man in the garden.

Before Mrs Parks can reply John and Michael enter R

John There's no-one there now. Are you quite sure you saw somebody?

Mrs Parks I ain't in the habit of throwing meself into the bushes just to ruin me hat.

Susan Did you recognize him—or didn't you?

Mrs Parks Well, not to say recognize—but I think it was Mr Watson from number thirty-seven. Worked for him a week I did after the Talbots left.

Helen has entered in time to hear the last sentence

Helen That's ridiculous. A glimpse—in the dark. How could you possibly recognize anybody?

Mrs Parks Because the light from the window was shining on his face.

Susan And he had a beard.

Helen So have hundreds of other people.

Susan Not in this road.

John What does that prove?

Michael Why not give the man a ring and see if he's home. If he is he couldn't have been in the garden because he hasn't had time to get back.

John We'll do nothing of the sort. For goodness' sake, let's keep a sense of proportion. Just because Mrs Parks thinks she saw somebody...

Mrs Parks I was pushed into the bushes.

John Exactly! You were knocked over by someone running away. You know very well that people take a short cut across the park at night when the gates are locked and climb over our wall to get out. We've complained to the police more than once.

Susan But the beard—the man at the dance!

John A coincidence.
Helen John's right—I think we're making trouble where there isn't any.
Michael So you're not going to do anything.
John None of us is going to do anything. (*Deliberately, to Mrs Parks*) None of us.
Mrs Parks Eh! Well I'm sure I'm not one for gossip.
Susan Yes—but—

She stops as Michael flashes her a look

Michael In that case we might as well be going.
Susan I—I'm ready.
John (*Who has not missed Michael's look*) What I said applies to you too, Michael. Just in case you have any ideas about calling at number thirty-seven.
Michael (*hotly*) But Mr Ferryman—
John Just what are you going to accuse him of doing? Trespassing? Assaulting Mrs Parks? Taking a photograph?
Susan Well I think he did.
John (*to Mrs Parks*) Would you swear that the man who knocked you over *was* Mr Watson?
Mrs Parks The truth, the whole truth, and nothing but?
John Exactly.
Mrs Parks Well—if you put it that way ...

John turns to Michael

Michael All right, Mr Ferryman. I get the message.
John Thank you (*To Mrs Parks*) And you?

The kettle whistles off L

Mrs Parks O.K. O.K.—That's my message. (*She goes to the kitchen door*) Tea!

Mrs Parks exits

Michael (*taking his case and Susan's and going towards the kitchen*) This way. I left my car by the garage.
Helen (*to Susan*) Are you sure you'll be all right?
Susan Quite sure. Now, Mother, don't start worrying.
Helen What time will you be back?
Susan Soon after midnight. And I promise not to disturb the neighbours. Goodnight, Mother.
Helen Goodnight, dear.

Michael and Susan exit

Mrs Parks (*putting her head round the door*) Tea's brewing. Anyone want a cuppa?
Helen No thanks.

Mrs Parks (*going to retrieve her hat*) Nearly forgot me one and only titfer. (*She moves back towards the kitchen*)
Helen Just one thing, Mrs Parks.
Mrs Parks What's that?
Helen What were you doing in the garden at eight o'clock?
Mrs Parks Came back for me money.
Helen You could have picked it up in the morning.
Mrs Parks Well, that's all right for you and me, Mrs Ferryman, but it ain't so good for my boy Joe. Likes to go to the club, he does, Thursday nights—just to have a drink with his pals.
Helen And *you* give him the money?
Mrs Parks Well I don't have no-one else to give it to—do I? I'll just have me cuppa and get along. Joe'll be waiting.

Mrs Parks exits to the kitchen

Helen (*looking after her*) I suppose we all need someone. (*Turning to John*) Oh, John.
John (*taking her in his arms*) Now, Helen, it's not like you to get so upset.
Helen Susan never did any harm to anyone. Why should anyone want to harm her?
John Maybe they don't. Maybe it's just a crank after all.

The front door bell rings

Damn! Can't we ignore it?
Helen You know we can't.

The bell rings again

Go and see who it is.
John (*resignedly*) All right.

He exits to the hall. Helen picks up the coffee tray and goes to the kitchen. There is the sound of voices in the hall. Mary Eastwood enters. She is a little older, a little more working-class than Helen. She has been a personable woman but ill-health and nerves have taken their toll. Her clothes are good quality but old-fashioned. She is in a temper verging on hysterics

Mary Where have they gone?

John follows her into the room

John Mrs Eastwood, however urgent—
Mary They drove past me as I came along the road. I called out to them but of course they didn't stop. Oh, no! It's all *her* now. I don't matter any more. I saw Michael sneaking out with his suitcase. They've run away together, haven't they? Well—where have they gone?

Helen has entered from the kitchen in time to hear the last question

Act I   13

Helen It's Michael's mother isn't it? Susan and Michael have gone to a dance at the Rugby Club.
Mary (*swinging round to face her*) You're lying!
John Mrs Eastwood!
Helen It's all right, John. (*To Mary*) Why do you think I'm lying?
Mary (*waving an envelope identical with the one Michael brought*) Because of this.
Helen (*tensely*) Where did you get this?
Mary It was half-way through your letter-box.
Helen (*slowly taking the envelope*) So that's why he came.
Mary What?
Helen Earlier on Mrs Parks saw someone in the garden.
Mary Who was it?
Helen We—we don't know. You—you haven't opened it. How do you know what's inside?
Mary It's just like the one Michael got. And I saw what was in *his*. A disgusting picture of your daughter.
John And your son!

During the next few speeches Helen opens the envelope, pulls the photograph out a little, glances at it, then pushes the picture back and puts the envelope on the divider

Mary She led him into it. That's what she's been doing all along—and you've encouraged her. Now they've gone away together.
Helen Just a minute, Mrs Eastwood. You actually think that Michael and Susan have eloped?
Mary You don't need a suitcase just to go to a dance!
Helen You do to this one. You take a suitcase of cast-off clothes for charity.
Mary (*uncertainly*) You're—you're covering up for them.
Helen It's the truth.
Mary And how do you explain that photograph?
John It's a fake.
Mary The one I saw looked genuine enough.
John If you want technical proof an expert would probably give it to you. We know it's a fake because *we* trust them.
Mary Are you suggesting I don't trust Michael?
John You're suggesting that—not me.
Mary (*after a moment, sinking on to the settee*) I—I don't know what to think. I only know that photograph could ruin Michael's career.
Helen (*sitting by her*) Surely you're exaggerating.
Mary You know what solicitors are like about scandal—whether it's true or not. And Michael isn't doing very well anyway. That's something else you're responsible for. Encouraging Michael to waste time with Susan. Letting them go out dancing when he should be studying. If his guardian heard about it he might stop his allowance—and I can't manage on my own.
Helen You could forbid Michael to come here.

Mary He wouldn't listen. He'd rather waste his time.

John Perhaps that's because you're forcing him into a career he doesn't want.

Mary (*hotly*) And what do you expect me to do? Let him join the police force like his father did? Let him be killed by a thug with a gun just like his father was? Do you think a police medal and a pension can take the place of a husband and a son.

Helen I'm sorry.

John Then if you want to protect Michael's job the best thing is to keep quiet.

Mary I—I suppose so.

John I've already told Susan and Michael not to say anything. Helen and I certainly won't. You're the only other person who knows.

Mary (*apprehensively*) No! I'm not the only person—I telephoned Ian.

John Ian?

Mary Michael's guardian. I didn't know what to do—Michael wouldn't tell me anything about the photograph or the phone call. Then I saw him putting his suitcase in the car and driving off. I thought they were running away—Well I had to talk to someone—and Ian's been like a father to Michael.

John Then he'll keep quiet for Michael's sake.

Mary No! No! You don't understand—Ian is a detective chief inspector. He couldn't keep it quiet.

There is a tap on the kitchen door and Mrs Parks pokes her head in

Mrs Parks Just thought I would let you know I'm going.

Helen Oh! Yes. Are you feeling all right?

Mrs Parks Barring a few bruises I wouldn't even let me husband look at even if I had one. (*She sees Mary and comes forward into the room*) Evening, Mrs Eastwood, heard about the excitement?

Mary Excitement?

Mrs Parks (*pointing*) The man out there—who attacked me.

John Mrs Parks!

Helen (*rising and going to Mrs Parks*) You'll miss your bus if you don't hurry. You've got your money?

Mrs Parks Safe and sound. (*She pats her pocket*)

Helen Then I'll see you in the morning.

Mrs Parks Okey-doke! (*She goes to the door and turns*) While I was having me tea I done some thinking. It *was* that Mr Watson from number thirty-seven what I saw, him that rented Talbot's house.

She exits through the kitchen

Mary You said you didn't know who it was.

Helen Would you take Mrs Park's word?

Mary All the same I think we ought to find out. I heard him on the phone when he spoke to Michael. I'd recognize his voice, I'm sure of it.

Act I 15

John I thought we'd decided to keep everything quiet. How can we if you start accusing people.
Mary I see that of course—but . . . Oh, I don't know.
John What's the name of Michael's guardian?
Mary Conway—Detective Chief Inspector Ian Conway.
John I think *he's* the immediate danger. Did you actually mention the photograph to him?
Mary I—I can't remember. I was worried. Everything was muddled. I said more about Michael and Susan running away—I just couldn't sit there waiting—and wondering—I asked him to come and see me.
Helen When he finds you gone what will he do?

The front doorbell rings

John I think that answers the question. Now we'll just have to play it as it comes.

He exits to the hall

Helen (*going to Mary; quietly and urgently*) Act as if you'd never seen the photograph. Concentrate on misunderstanding the telephone call and elopement. For Michael's sake.
Mary I—I'll do my best.
John (*ushering in Ian*) Here *is* Detective Chief Inspector Conway.

Ian is in his middle forties, shrewd, tenacious and deceptively matter-of-fact in his manner. A steady and sturdy man with a wry sense of humour. He is not in the best of tempers

Ian (*to Helen*) My apologies for intruding, Mrs Ferryman.
Helen Not at all.
Ian (*to Mary*) Well, Mary, I guessed I'd find you here.
Mary I thought you weren't coming.
Ian I did the best I could. I can't just drop everything every time you phone.
Mary I'm sorry. It was all a mistake.
Ian A mistake!

John gestures for Ian to sit and he does so

You said something about a phone call. Surely you know whether there was one or not?
Mary Of course there was. But I only heard part of it—and—and I must have misunderstood.
Ian And the suitcase you said Michael took with him—was that a mistake too?
Mary Yes! No! I mean . . .
Helen Aren't you being a little severe, Inspector?
Ian Dr Ferryman, I'm a very busy man. My desk is piled with reports I'll

have to— (*He stops suddenly, then relaxes*) Yes, perhaps you're right. Will someone please tell me what happened.
Helen It's so simple there's really nothing to tell. Mrs Eastwood put certain isolated incidents together—and decided that Susan and Michael were planning to elope.
Ian And what in fact were they doing?
Helen Going to a local dance in aid of Oxfam, to which the admission was a suitcase of old clothing.
Ian There's no doubt about it?
Helen None.
Ian That being so—if you'll excuse me, I'll get back to the station. (*Rising. To Mary*) I'll drop you at home on the way.
Mary No! I mean—Mr Ferryman said he'd walk round with me—I need some fresh air—I—I haven't been sleeping . . .
John (*taking his cue*) Oh, yes—yes—I was just about to get my coat when you arrived. I'll get it now.

He exits to the hall leaving the door open

Ian Then I'll just say goodnight.
Helen If you could spare a few minutes now you're here I'd like a word with you. (*As Ian hesitates*) I think it's important.
Ian Very well—I'll wait.

John enters from the hall, putting on his coat

John If you're ready, Mrs Eastwood . . .
Mary (*moving towards the door—as she passes Ian*) I'm sorry for being such a nuisance to you.
Ian (*kindly*) Forget it, Mary. I'd rather have a false alarm than think you weren't going to come to me at all. I'll call round to see you tomorrow.
Mary Thank you.

Mary exits to the hall. John follows but stops in the doorway

John (*to Ian*) I'll only be a few minutes but in case you've gone before I get back I'll say goodnight.
Ian Goodnight, Mr Ferryman.

John exits

Helen (*uncertainly*) Would—would you like a drink?
Ian Dr Ferryman, as I said, I'm rather pressed—
Helen I'm sorry. (*Making up her mind. Facing him*) Mr Conway, what is the position of a woman whose husband is reported to be dead?
Ian Reported? How reported?
Helen By the French police—after an inquest.
Ian (*rather puzzled*) She's a widow.
Helen She can re-marry?
Ian She can do anything a widow can do.
Helen But if the first husband turns out to be alive?

Act I

Ian If you're thinking of bigamy—I doubt if the charge would hold.
Helen Why not?
Ian She acted in good faith—and the law doesn't punish people for its own mistakes.
Helen But which man is her husband?
Ian That's more difficult. I think the official report would act like a divorce. But that's only my opinion. The churches might not agree.
Helen And anything the wife inherited?
Ian I think she has a legal claim to it.
Helen And morally?
Ian You might feel obliged to pay it back.
Helen Me! I didn't say it was my problem.
Ian No—of course you didn't. Is that all?
Helen I'm sorry if I've asked too many questions.
Ian (*smiling*) It makes a change. It's usually the other way about.
Helen There *is* just one other thing. Michael and Susan seem very fond of each other. The question of an engagement might come up.
Ian There'll be no objection from me as long as it doesn't interfere with his studies. What you really want to know is—how's Mary going to take it?
Helen Well—yes.
Ian You'll have trouble. I don't know if Michael's told you but he was only a few weeks old when his father was killed. We were on watch together and cornered a young tear-away. When he drew a gun on me Michael's father jumped him. I've always believed he saved my life. Afterwards, when I went to see Mary, she was clinging to the baby as if he was all she had left. And that's the way it's been ever since.
Helen Surely something can be done.
Ian Such as what? Every time Michael tries to go his own way she has some kind of nervous break-down. As a doctor you may be able to think of something. I can't—I only wish I could. I'm not married and I suppose I've grown to look on Michael as my own son. Now, I really must be going.

As Ian moves towards the hall John enters

The telephone rings

Helen (*moving towards the telephone*) Oh John, would you see Mr Conway out?
John (*holding the door open*) Of course.
Helen Goodnight, Mr Conway—and thank you.
Ian Goodnight.

Ian and John exit to the hall

Helen (*on the telephone*) Hello! ... Yes? Dr Ferryman speaking.... There's still no reaction.... Very well, I'll be along in about a quarter of an hour.

Helen rings off and goes towards the hall door

John re-enters having taken off his coat. They meet half way and John puts his arms round her

John Don't say you're going out.
Helen I have to.
John What did you want to talk to the police about?
Helen (*evading his eyes*) I was talking to Michael's guardian. I wanted his reaction to the idea of Susan and Michael getting engaged.
John And?
Helen He was in favour.
John I wonder what his reaction would have been to that photograph?
Helen Oh, John. (*She clings to him*) You don't think that Mr Watson is responsible, do you?
John Why should he be? He doesn't know us. We don't know him.
Helen No—no of course not. (*She breaks away*) I have a patient waiting.
John How long will you be?
Helen I don't know. (*She looks at her watch*) A quarter to nine. It's a difficult case—but I shouldn't be more than an hour.
John Don't worry, dear. Things'll work out all right. You'll see.

Helen exits

John picks up the envelope containing the photograph from the divider, weighs it thoughtfully then slaps it down angrily as if coming to a decision. He goes to the telephone and opens the directory

John Tad ... Tag ... Tal ... Talbot, thirty-seven Parkside Avenue. (*He dials the number*) Mr Watson? ... This is John Ferryman and I—— ... (*Angrily*) I'm coming to see you now. ... Never mind how I traced you. ... (*Threateningly*) I listened to you last time. This time you listen to me!

CURTAIN

ACT II

Scene 1

A corner of the sitting-room/study of 37 Parkside Avenue. The time is still 8.45 pm. The action is continuous with Act I

As the house is rented the room reflects nothing of Mr Watson's character. To the right is a settee and above it is a drinks table. There are french windows to the back and below to the left is a writing table and two chairs, a standard lamp, and further a fireplace, telephone table and an archway to the hall.

Mr Watson is speaking on the telephone. He is in his early forties, good looking, well built with a luxurious beard. His voice is educated and his easy charm conceals a cynical ruthlessness. Stretched out on the settee is Rita Davies. She is a glamorous woman of twenty-five with striking blonde hair and is by no means as silly as she seems. They are both rather dishevelled and it is obvious that the telephone call interrupted a 'session' on the settee

Mr Watson (*on the telephone*) I *am* listening, Mr Ferryman. I'm listening very carefully. I haven't made arrangements to meet you before, simply because I've only just got the proof you wanted. . . . It's no use coming now because I have someone with me. And I'm sure you don't want to discuss your business in front of a third party. . . . (*Firmly*) I'll see you in a quarter of an hour, Mr Ferryman, *not before*. . . . Mr Ferryman. . . . Mr Ferryman! (*He slams down the receiver*) Damn and blast!
Rita Who was that?
Mr Watson A visitor.
Rita Trouble?
Mr Watson Not really. In fact it's a piece of business I've been looking forward to.
Rita Paying business?
Mr Watson Of course. But more important, I'm really going to enjoy doing it.
Rita Then what are you worried about?
Mr Watson It's come to a head sooner than I anticipated. (*He sits beside Rita on the settee and puts his arms round her*) You'll have to do the deliveries tonight.
Rita I've done them before.
Mr Watson Not on your own.
Rita Then put them off until tomorrow.
Mr Watson Too risky. I don't want the stuff lying round here. Besides junkies get nervous when supplies aren't on time—and when they're

nervous they're liable to do silly things. Like talking too much. You shouldn't have any trouble. You know the contacts—and they know you.

He stands up and pulls Rita to her feet

Come on—playtime's over.

As she stands up she leans against him and they go into a long kiss. Eventually he breaks away

Pity ... but ... (*He turns her towards the hall and slaps her bottom*) Go and make yourself respectable.
Rita Just for you, darling. Just for you.

Rita picks up her handbag from the desk and exits through the archway. Mr Watson straightens his tie, puts on his jacket and smoothes his hair. The telephone rings

Mr Watson (*snatching up the receiver; sharply*) Yes! ... Oh! ... (*Easily*) No, I'm afraid Mr and Mrs Talbot are away.... For at least six months. I've rented the house from them.... Sorry I can't help you. Perhaps the agent.... Not at all.

Mr Watson replaces the receiver, opens a drawer in the desk, takes out a pair of white cotton gloves, puts them on and then takes from the drawer three small white packets, sealed with red sealing-wax, and a handbag identical with the one Rita has just taken off

Rita comes storming in

Rita (*slamming her handbag down on the desk*) So that's the game!
Mr Watson (*baffled*) What is?
Rita Skipping out. Midnight flitting.
Mr Watson You must be mad.
Rita Then what are those cases for? In the spare room.
Mr Watson Oh, those. They're always packed. One of these days I may have to move fast and I wouldn't want to leave anything personal behind.
Rita Does that include me?
Mr Watson (*rising*) Darling, if I go—you go—naturally.
Rita (*still suspicious*) How many plane tickets have you got? One or two? Perhaps I'd better check.
Mr Watson No need. (*He takes two plane tickets out of his pocket*) Here they are—Mr Cowley—Mrs Cowley.
Rita That's not us.
Mr Watson It will be when we set off.
Rita And afterwards?
Mr Watson I'll make an honest woman of you.
Rita You mean—you'll keep your promise—you'll marry me—legitimate?

Act II, Scene 1   21

Mr Watson Legitimate! (*Taking a passport out of the desk drawer*) Here you are—all sealed and signed. No trouble at all if you know the right people.
Rita (*reading the passport; dreamily*) Mr and Mrs Cowley (*Practically*) And what about our money?
Mr Watson *Our* money?
Rita Well I've helped you to get it, haven't I? Is it in those cases?
Mr Watson No, my sweet. It's in a very safe place.
Rita The safe-deposit box?
Mr Watson Exactly. (*He pats his breast pocket*) And I have the key right here.
Rita (*close to him, coaxing*) You wouldn't let Rita keep it for you?
Mr Watson You're damn right I wouldn't.

Rita reaches for his face, claws out, but Mr Watson puts his arms round her and they go into a long kiss. Slowly Rita relaxes

Rita (*as they break away*) You're a real bastard.
Mr Watson How did you guess? (*He suddenly notices the time on the travelling-clock*) Hey! You'll have to get a move on or you'll miss the first contact. Nine-thirty at Harry's bar.
Rita I know.

Rita goes into the hall, returning almost immediately, putting on a mackintosh, with a large inside pocket

Mr Watson, still wearing the cotton gloves, puts the packets into the handbag

Mr Watson (*as Rita returns*) One packet to each contact and cash on the nail. Any contact not on time don't wait—go on to the next.
Rita I know all that.
Mr Watson Maybe you do. But this is the first time you've been on your own and if you slip up you won't get a second chance.
Rita Don't you trust me?
Mr Watson If I didn't you wouldn't be going (*As Rita reaches out to pick up the handbag containing the packets*) Don't touch that!
Rita No need to shout.
Mr Watson (*quieter*) Until you've got your gloves on.

Rita takes the gloves out of the mackintosh pocket, puts them on and picks up the bag containing the packets. As she turns towards the archway

Mr Watson (*pointing to Rita's own bag*) And don't forget this.
Rita O.K. . . . O.K. (*She turns back, picks up the handbag and slips it into the inside pocket of her mackintosh*)
Mr Watson In case of trouble dump the one with the drugs—(*pointing to the bag under Rita's arm*)—and start carrying your own. (*Indicating the bag in the mackintosh pocket*) Understand?
Rita Do you think I'm dumb or something? (*She flutters her eyelashes*) Does the great big policeman want to look in my silly old handbag?
Mr Watson Don't underestimate the police.

Rita I've met them before.

Mr Watson Well you don't want to meet them again. I'll ring you just before eleven to see if everything's gone all right.

Rita Can't I come back here? After all—we were interrupted.

Mr Watson (*half putting his arm round her then stopping*) No. No, it's best you keep away.

He relents as Rita puts on an appealing expression

Oh, all right—I'll let you know when I ring.

As Rita turns towards the archway he grabs her arm and steers her towards the french windows

This way out.

Rita exits, blowing him a kiss

Mr Watson closes the curtains, then goes to the telephone and dials

(*On the telephone*) Harry? ... Rita's on her way. Keep an eye on her and make sure she doesn't do anything silly. And this'll be the last time. She's getting a bit of a nuisance. A new middleman's taking over. That's all you need to know. ... Split? Rita? She daren't. ... Don't worry about me. By the time she finds out I won't be here. (*He rings off*)

Moving quickly he drops the tickets, passport and gloves into the desk drawer. Moving the electric fire to one side he reaches inside the chimney and brings out a small metal box which he places on the desk. The doorbell rings. He takes an envelope out of the box and places it also in the drawer, and closes both box and drawer. The doorbell rings again. With a quick look round he goes to answer it

(*Off*) You'll gain nothing by being impatient Mr Ferryman. I told you a quarter of an hour.

John (*off*) Out of my way!

He enters quickly—obviously in a temper. Mr Watson follows him in

Mr Watson This isn't very wise of you. Mr Ferryman.

John (*turning to face him*) It wasn't very wise of you to be seen in someone else's garden.

Mr Watson An unfortunate accident. Mrs Parks recognized me, then?

John More or less.

Mr Watson That explains how you traced me—but not why you chose to disobey my instructions to wait until I phoned you again. What's so urgent?

John (*slamming envelope containing the photograph down on the desk in front of Mr Watson*) This!

Mr Watson (*taking the photograph out and looking at it*) Oh, very tasty, if you like that sort of thing. Your step-daughter, isn't it?

Act II, Scene 1   23

John You know damn well it is!
Mr Watson Really, Mr Ferryman. Anyone would think you were accusing me of something. (*He puts the photograph on the desk*)
John Do you deny leaving this at my house?
Mr Watson I left an envelope. What was in it I have no idea.
John You're a liar.
Mr Watson Mr Ferryman. I made it quite clear at our first meeting. I'm just an agent. My clients pay me well to carry out their instructions and keep my mouth shut. I was told to deliver an envelope and I did as I was told.
John Do you think the police will believe that?
Mr Watson Why not try them? There's the phone. There's the photograph. Go ahead.

John makes a slight movement as if he is going to do just that

(*Quickly*) But I should warn you that if you do—my client isn't going to like it.
John (*scornfully*) Your client!
Mr Watson No doubt he still has the negatives—and I believe there's quite a market for this type of art.

John (*taking hold of Mr Watson's jacket*) I'll break every bone—
Mr Watson (*easily breaking John's grip but keeping hold of his wrists*) I wouldn't try violence, Mr Ferryman. You're not really the type.

He pushes John away with so much force that he falls on to settee

John (*trembling with anger*) If I ever see one more photograph like that I promise that you—and your client—will end up in prison—no matter what it costs.
Mr Watson (*calmly*) I'll see that your message reaches him. Now as long as you're here we might as well get down to business. You asked for proof that Mr Lovat—your—er—wife's real husband—was still alive, (*He takes a snapshot and a diary out of a box*) Here it is. This snapshot, for instance—not as sensational as the photograph you so kindly brought—but interesting all the same. (*He realizes John is taking no notice*) Mr Ferryman!
John I've nothing more to say to you.
Mr Watson On the contrary—you have a lot more to say. Unless of course you're prepared to give up all the easy living you can enjoy on your wife's money. That comfortable modern bungalow. That junior partnership. Because you know where the money came from. Those shares your wife inherited from Mr Lovat.
John The shares were Helen's.
Mr Watson They weren't transferred to your wife until *after* Mr Lovat was presumed dead. I checked.
John I don't understand.
Mr Watson Then there are aspects of the situation which affect *Doctor* Ferryman personally. Such as living in sin for twelve months. The

B.M.A. are rather old fashioned about things like that. And no-one knows just how your step-daughter would react. She might even choose to leave you and join her real father.

John All right! All right! There's no need to go on.

Mr Watson Mr Lovat used to carry that in his wallet—but strangely enough it shows no sign of the fire which was supposed to have destroyed the car with him inside. You recognize the people of course. In fact you may possibly have seen a snapshot like it before. Mrs Ferryman also had a copy.

John It's Helen and Simon Lovat. But this doesn't prove he's still alive.

Mr Watson Not by itself—but if you'll turn it over you'll find two signatures. Faded a little after twenty years but still clear enough for our purpose. I believe the snap was taken the day they became engaged and they both signed it. Helen Sinclair and Simon Lovat.

John I don't see what——

Mr Watson You will. (*He hands the open diary to John*) Just compare the signature with this one. (*He picks up a magnifying-glass and hands it to John*) Perhaps you'd like to use this.

John (*after examination*) They're—identical.

Mr Watson And where is the second signature written?

John In a diary.

Mr Watson For——

John For this year.

Mr Watson And Mr Lovat—er—died—some years ago!

Almost frantically John examines both signatures again. Mr Watson watches with half a smile

John (*after a pause*) It's impossible. The police . . . The courts . . .

Mr Watson . . . made a very natural mistake. The body *was too badly burned* for a definite physical identification. They had to rely on circumstantial evidence—and that evidence was faked.

John But why did Mr Lovat want everyone to believe he was dead?

Mr Watson Because of a natural reluctance to go to prison. The car he was driving contained a large quantity of drugs.

John Then what's to stop me telling the police he's still alive?

Mr Watson (*patiently*) Mr Ferryman, I'm afraid you still haven't fully appreciated the situation. If you tell the police my client may go to prison for a few years—but by the same action you would lose your wife—her money—and your step-daughter, of whom you seem to be very fond. Perhaps a little fonder than might seem respectable. (*Picking up the photograph*) Not that I blame you after seeing this.

John (*rising quickly, and grasping a candlestick and swinging at Mr Watson's head. Strongly*) You filthy minded——

Mr Watson (*grasping candlestick and wrenching it from John's hand*) Mr Ferryman, I've warned you once.

For a moment they stand facing each other. Then John turns away and Mr Watson puts the candlestick down on the desk

Act II, Scene 1   25

Mr Watson And now we've got the position quite clear—shall we discuss terms?
John Terms?
Mr Watson My client will accept five thousand pounds to remain officially dead.
John (*staggered*) Five thousand pounds! Even if I was willing to pay I haven't got that kind of money.
Mr Watson I'm sure your wife would give it to you. Of course she wouldn't have to know what it was for because I doubt if she would submit to——
John —blackmail!
Mr Watson I was going to say "pressure".
John I've never asked Helen for money.
Mr Watson Oh, no?
John She *lent* me the capital to buy a partnership. It'll all be paid back.
Mr Watson How very noble. (*He sits on the settee*) Still, we're not beaten yet. As a partner in an accountancy firm I imagine that a lot more than five thousand pounds passes through your hands.
John Are you suggesting that I should rob my own firm?
Mr Watson I'm not suggesting anything. I'm simply putting forward my client's proposal. What you do about it is your own affair.
John I—I'll have to think it over.
Mr Watson (*rising and going to the desk*) Of course. But don't take too long. If I don't hear from you by Wednesday my instructions are to forward these—(*indicating the snapshot and the diary*)—to the police. Anonymously, of course.
John (*standing and facing him*) But that would mean——
Mr Watson —trouble for you and Mrs—Doctor—Ferryman.
John And prison for Simon Lovat.
Mr Watson I doubt it, Mr Ferryman. You see the police know where *you* are. But Mr Lovat has had several years to build up another identity in another country. Somehow I don't think the police would ever find him.

John opens his mouth to say something, then swings on his heels and exits through the archway. The front door slams

Mr Watson follows him to the archway, looks after him smiling cynically then returns to the desk, puts the diary and snapshot back into the box and the box inside the chimney. The telephone rings

Mr Watson (*on the telephone*) Yes?... Speaking.... You didn't get your supplies because you weren't at the contact point last night.... That's your problem.... Yes, I still have it but now it'll cost you double.... Special delivery and special risk—that's why. Do you want it or not? ... I'll be there in half-an-hour. (*He rings off*)

Using his handkerchief he takes a further packet from the drawer and slips it into his pocket. He then switches off the standard lamp and goes into the hall. We see him putting his coat on. He switches off the hall light. We hear the front door slam. The only light now is the glow of the fire. This is faded to a complete blackout to denote the passage of about an hour. The clock in the hall chimes the quarter-hour—10.15 p.m.—and the firelight is faded in. There is a sharp crack from the french window. The curtains part a little and a dark figure is silhouetted against faint moonlight. The figure, unrecognizable in the dim light, switches on a torch. The beam waves a little then comes to rest on the desk. As the figure moves forward there is a sound of the front door opening. With a startled gasp the intruder switches off the torch and takes refuge behind the curtains. She has hardly done so when the light goes on in the hall. Mr Watson is seen crossing the archway taking off his coat. After a moment he enters and switches on the standard lamp. Leisurely, he goes to the table and pours himself a drink. He is just raising it to his lips when he notices the curtains bulging. Quietly and quickly he puts down the glass, crosses to the window and pulls the curtains back revealing Mrs Eastwood. She tries to escape but he grabs her wrists and pulls her, struggling and protesting, into the room

Mr Watson And who exactly are you?

As Mary struggles

Don't do that. You'll only get hurt.

Mary I want the negatives that made that filthy photograph!

Mr Watson What photograph?

Mary It's no use pretending you don't know about it. I recognized your voice.

Mr Watson You did what?

Mary I was listening on the extension when you phoned my son. Then I spoke to you myself.

Mr Watson You spoke to me! (*He looks at the telephone. Realizing*) You were the woman who wanted the Talbots. That was very clever of you.

Mary I'll do anything to protect Michael.

Mr Watson Including house-breaking apparently. How did you get in?

Mary I broke the lock on the window.

Mr Watson (*letting go of her wrists and glancing behind the curtain*) What with?

Mary (*taking out of her pocket a short, strong, all-metal screwdriver*) This.

Mr Watson The complete cracksman. I'd better have these. (*He takes the torch and screwdriver and drops them in the drawer*) I take it you're Mrs Eastwood?

Mary Yes. (*As Mr Watson picks up the telephone*) What are you doing?

Mr Watson What every householder should do when he catches a burglar —phoning the police.

The telephone call is a bluff. He does not put the receiver to his ear but holds it in such a way that he can use one finger to keep the rest depressed, standing so that his body is between Mary and the telephone. Though apparently intent on the call he watches Mary out of the corner of his eye. He begins to dial

Mary If you do I'll tell them why I came.

Act II, Scene 1   27

Mr Watson To steal some photographs which you think I have. I doubt if the police will believe that.
Mary (*grabbing his arm*) You're not going to do it.

Suddenly Mary goes berserk. The force of her attack is such that Mr Watson staggers back. She grabs the telephone cord and tears it away

I told you I'd do anything to protect Michael.

As they stand facing each other across the desk, both see the photograph which John has left. Both dive for it but Mary gets hold of it first

Now, what have you got to say?
Mr Watson (*controlling himself with an effort*) Only that it's a great pity you found it. It's going to cost you a lot of money.
Mary Money?
Mr Watson Unless you want me to send copies to all your friends—to your son's employers——
Mary You wouldn't do that!
Mr Watson No?
Mary What did Michael ever do to you? Why do you want to ruin him?
Mr Watson But I don't—unless you force me to by refusing to buy the photographs.
Mary How—how much do you want?
Mr Watson Five hundred pounds.
Mary But I haven't got that kind of money.
Mr Watson For the sake of your son's future—don't say that.
Mary You'll have to give me time.
Mr Watson Until next Wednesday.
Mary I can't. It's impossible.
Mr Watson Next Wednesday, Mrs Eastwood. I'm sure you'll manage it somehow. In the meantime—(*with a quick movement he jerks the photograph out of Mary's hand*)—I'll keep this.

Mary tries to get it back but he slips it between the pages of the telephone directory and places both hands firmly on top. For a moment they stand face to face

I think you'd better go the way you came.
Mary (*she swings round, goes to the french window and turns*) You'll give me the negative as well?
Mr Watson Of course.
Mary How do I know I can trust you?
Mr Watson You don't really have much choice, do you, Mrs Eastwood?

Mary exits, leaving window slightly open behind the curtain. The clock in the hall chimes the half hour

Mr Watson remembers the drink which he poured before Mary came, picks it up and is sipping it meditatively when the front doorbell rings. He looks puzzled, then his face clears

Rita! Oh, well . . .

He puts his drink down and exits through the archway as the front door bell rings again. There is a slight pause then voices off—protesting—demanding. Helen enters quickly. She wears an old mackintosh slightly wet and a head-scarf drawn forward to conceal her face. She has pushed past Mr Watson who has had no chance to recognize her

Mr Watson (*off*) Hey! Just a minute. What the devil——

Mr Watson enters

(*As he enters*) Whoever you are I hope you have a good explanation for bursting in at half-past ten at night!

Helen (*removing the scarf and turning to face him*) No, Simon. The explanation will have to come from you.

Mr Watson (*with surprise and caution*) Helen!

Helen I was married to you for quite a long time. You didn't really think dark glasses, a beard and a bottle of hair-dye would fool me. Who was killed instead of you?

Mr Watson A friend.

Helen Also wanted by the police?

Mr Watson Of course.

Helen And you planted the evidence?

Mr Watson Why waste a chance like that? So here I am—alive and very well. What are you going to do about it?

Helen What I promised to do if you ever came back.

Mr Watson You wouldn't dare.

Helen Are you sure?

Mr Watson You've re-married. You sold the shares. Which makes you a bigamist and a thief.

Helen Oh, no.

Mr Watson Then there's Susan. She's grown up. She's a young woman with a lot to lose. I wonder how she'd react to the news that Simon Lovat was still alive.

Helen She's your daughter!

Mr Watson No! You took her away from me a long time ago. You weren't satisfied with being a judge and jury. You climbed on your little pedestal and tried to be God.

Helen I did what I had to do.

Mr Watson You enjoyed it. No, Mrs Simon Lovat, Bachelor of Medicine lording it over her failure of a husband who had more skill in his little finger than you have in your whole body. You forget that even the worst human beings need a little pride—a little bit of respect. You turned me into a puppet.

Helen Believe me, Simon. I never intended that.

Mr Watson Do this! Do that! Drop all your friends——

Act II, Scene 1   29

Helen Friends! Scroungers you mean!
Mr Watson Go away, you said—and I had to go. Well now you know what it feels like to be on the other end of the string. I stood in that garden tonight and watched you through the window and enjoyed it.
Helen So that's why——
Mr Watson It was worth the risk of coming back to watch your sanctimonious little world begin to crumble. I was God—not you.
Helen Not any more, Simon. I'll give you two thousand pounds for the photographs and the negatives.
Mr Watson So now you're singing a different tune?
Helen Not because I'm afraid of anything you can do to me—but because I don't want Susan to find out the kind of man I picked for her father.
Mr Watson Damn you! You're not getting away with a miserable two thousand pounds. What about the fortune you got from the shares?
Helen The shares were mine.
Mr Watson I bought them.
Helen I redeemed them with *my* money. If you want to claim them you'll have to come out in the open and fight. And if you do that I'll hand over to the police the evidence I should have given them years ago.
Mr Watson Evidence?
Helen Prescriptions you forged in my name to get drugs. Letters from the little floosies who used to do your dirty work until you had them hooked and then dropped them—I can prove it, Simon, every bit of it.
Mr Watson (*strongly*) All right! All right!
Helen (*producing a cheque and letter envelope from her pocket*) Here's a cheque for two thousand pounds.
Mr Watson (*scornfully*) A cheque!
Helen An open one. And a letter to the bank. Just as good as money.
Mr Watson (*quietly but intensely*) Damn you to hell!

He almost snatches the cheque, letter and envelope, examines them then takes an envelope out of the drawer and slams it down on the desk. Helen opens it, takes out a 35 mm negative which she holds up to the light, then satisfied, sets fire to the envelope and contents using a cigarette lighter taken from her pocket. She drops the burning envelope into the waste-paper bin. Mr Watson puts the cheque into his pocket

Helen But that isn't the whole story—is it, Simon?
Mr Watson (*tensely*) What?
Helen You didn't go to all this trouble just for revenge.
Mr Watson I've told you——
Helen Blackmail. That's what you had in mind wasn't it? But if you'd come out with it right away you knew I wouldn't give you a penny. These —(*indicating the bin*)—were just to soften me up. (*Facing him*) Isn't that right?
Mr Watson Surely it's worth a few thousands to protect your career, your marriage—(*meaningly*)—your daughter?
Helen No!

Mr Watson Remember, if I stay "dead" for another twelve months you can get a quiet divorce for desertion.
Helen And how many times during that twelve months will you be back for more money?
Mr Watson I promise——
Helen (*scornfully*) You promise.
Mr Watson I can destroy everything you've built up.
Helen Not as long as I have the prescriptions and the letters.
Mr Watson Don't bank on it. All I have to do is to show that I'm alive. And I can do that without letting the police get their hands on me. You never thought of that, did you?
Helen I'll pay you at the end of the year.
Mr Watson By that time your precious John Ferryman will have got his hands on your money and left you flat.
Helen I'll give you the evidence as well.
Mr Watson How do I know you've still got it? How do I know you didn't destroy it when you heard I was dead?
Helen You don't. But isn't it worth waiting a year to make sure?
Mr Watson You're bluffing.
Helen It's my last offer. I advise you to accept it. (*She swings on her heels, goes to the archway, turns*) I warn you, Simon. You tried to ruin my life once before. Now I've built up another life with Susan—and someone I love. Don't try to ruin that—because I'll see you dead first!

Helen exits

Mr Watson follows as far as the archway, looking after her. The front door slams. With a muttered curse he turns back into the room and picks up the telephone. As he begins to dial he realizes that the line is dead. He picks up the loose cord and slams it down again

Mr Watson Blast that neurotic bitch.

He goes quickly into the hall, returns immediately struggling into his coat and takes a handful of change out of his pocket and stands by the standard lamp, obviously looking for a two pence piece. Finding it he switches the lamp off and is turning towards the archway when the curtain billows slightly and the gleam of moonlight catches his eye

That bloody lock!

He moves to the window but stops a pace or two away sensing something. Staring at the curtains

Who's there? Who the hell's there?

And as Mr Watson reaches out and drags the curtains open there is—

a Black-out and quick CURTAIN

Scene 2

The Ferrymans' lounge. As Act I

The time is 9.30 a.m. on the following morning. The sun is shining brightly. The dining-table is set for breakfast for three, including a packet of cereals

When the CURTAIN *rises the stage is empty*

John enters R. *He is edgy, tense and in a hurry. He carries his jacket under his arm and is fixing his tie*

John (*dropping his jacket on to the settee*) Helen!—Helen!

Helen enters left carrying a coffee-pot

Helen, do you know what time it is?
Helen (*going to the table and pouring out two cups of coffee. Calmly*) Half-past-nine.
John (*putting on his jacket, having fixed his tie*) Why on earth didn't you wake me?
Helen Because you were asleep—and because you're not due anywhere until eleven-thirty. Good morning.
John What? Oh, good morning, dear.

He gives her a quick kiss, holds her chair for her to sit down and himself sits to the left of the table. Helen passes him a cup of coffee. He helps himself to cereal and they proceed with breakfast

Helen How's the scheme?
John Finished.
Helen What time did you come to bed?
John After midnight.
Helen Did Susan say anything when she came in?
John I didn't see her.
Helen Surely she knew you were still up?
John I—I expect I was still out.
Helen At midnight?
John I had a headache. It was a lovely night.
Helen Wasn't it raining?
John Not when I went out. (*A little irritably*) I just went for a stroll.
Helen (*soothingly*) Of course, dear.

Mrs Parks enters L, *carrying a toast-rack*

Mrs Parks (*brightly*) Here you are, Mr Ferryman. Nice hot fresh toast.
John Thank you.
Mrs Parks And how about an egg and a couple of rashers?
John No thank you. Just toast.

Mrs Parks Never could abide this cornflake and coffee lark myself. Roughage that's all it is—roughage. Now my boy Joe——
Helen (*over-riding*) Thank you, Mrs Parks.
Mrs Parks Oh! Okey-doke.

She exits cheerfully to the kitchen

John (*who has been holding himself back with difficulty, bursts out*) Helen! If you don't stop that woman . . .
Helen (*calmly*) Are you quite sure it's all her fault.
John (*relaxing*) Yes—you may be right at that.

Susan enters quickly, R, wearing a fluffy negligée

Susan (*going straight to window*) What's all the hu-ha in the avenue—I've been watching from my bedroom? Policemen all over the place. Now they're calling at all the houses.
Helen (*joining her at window*) Policemen?
Susan Well, detectives. (*Pointing*) There!
Helen He doesn't look any more like a detective than the next man.
John (*strongly*) Will you stop peering out?
Helen John!
John If you spy on people—they spy on you.
Susan (*hotly*) No-one's spying.
Helen Susan! Sit down and get on with your breakfast.
Susan But, Mother——
Helen Please, Susan.

Unwillingly, Susan sits at the table and helps herself to cereals. Helen also sits. There is a moment's awkward silence

John I apologize——I'm sorry.

Mrs Parks bursts in L, carrying a tray

Mrs Parks (*excitedly*) Have you heard what's happened. That Mr Watson in number thirty-seven—he's been found dead. All battered and bloody the milkman said.
Helen Oh, no!
Susan So that's it!
John Oh, for God's sake.

John moves quickly down R, takes a cigarette out of his case, strikes several matches before he succeeds in lighting it, then drops into the armchair. Helen remains frozen. Meanwhile, Susan and Mrs Parks carry on regardless

Mrs Parks Well!
Susan Go on, Parky.
Mrs Parks Lying in the road all night he was.
Susan You mean—in this road?

Act II, Scene 2

Mrs Parks That's right, dear. In the gutter outside his own door.
Susan But he couldn't have been. Not all night.
Helen Please!

Susan and Mrs Parks look at each other in surprise

Mrs Parks What have I said?
Susan (*overlapping*) Mother, what's the matter with you?
Helen That's no way to talk about murder.
Susan Who said it was murder? And how do you expect me to talk about it? (*The front doorbell rings*) We didn't even know the man. That'll be the detective. Well I'm going to finish my breakfast in the kitchen.

She exits

The doorbell rings again

Mrs Parks Shall I answer it?
Helen No—no, I'll go.

Helen crosses to door R. *As she passes John she hesitates as if going to say something, then continues and exits*

As soon as she has gone John gets up and helps himself to a drink with unsteady hands. Meanwhile, Mrs Parks has been placing the crockery, etc., on the tray

Susan puts her head through the hatch

Susan Bring the coffee and toast, Parky. I'm starving.
Mrs Parks Okey-doke.

She makes sure the coffee and toast are on the tray and puts it through the hatch, then exits L. *Susan removes the tray from the hatch and closes the door, leaving a small gap. Helen re-enters followed by Inspector Conway. With an effort John pulls himself together*

Ian Good morning, Mr Ferryman.
Helen I take it this is an official visit?
Ian I'm afraid so.
John We expected someone lower down the hierarchy.
Ian Expected?
John (*indicating the window*) Your activities haven't gone unnoticed. Why have we been honoured?
Ian (*casually*) Oh, I still like to do some of the leg work. I suppose you'll have heard then that a Mr Watson from along the avenue has met with an accident.
Helen We heard he was dead.

Ian Did you hear anything unusual last night—say between half-past ten and midnight?
Helen I was——
John We were in bed.

As John says this he moves between Helen and Ian so that the latter cannot see her look of surprise

Ian One of your neighbours saw a light downstairs at half-past eleven.
John I was working in the study. Perhaps it was later than I thought. Is it important?
Ian Not as long as you didn't go out.
John We didn't.
Ian And you heard nothing at all?
John Nothing.
Ian Another neighbour says she was awakened around midnight by the sound of voices and car doors slamming. The car was outside your house. One of the voices was Susan's—the other probably Michael's.
John So that's why you came personally.
Ian I've told you why. (*To Helen*) I'd like a word with Susan.
Helen Before you do I want to know what this is all about.
Ian Just routine.
Helen I don't believe you. A—a stranger meets with an accident—and you want to know where we were—what we were doing. Is this Mr Watson dead or not?
Ian He is.
Helen And how did he die?
Ian We're not certain.
Helen (*moving towards the door* R) Then perhaps until you are——
Ian Mrs Ferryman.
John I think we have a right to know what is—uncertain—about his death.
Ian (*after a moment*) It might not have been altogether natural.
Helen You mean—murder?
Ian I didn't say that. It could still have been an accident.
John Like hit and run?
Ian What made you think of that?
John Mrs Parks said the body was battered—and lying in the gutter.
Ian Mrs Parks?
Helen Our daily help. She heard it from the milkman.
John Is that what happened?
Ian Until we get the result of the post-mortem I wouldn't like to say. (*To Helen*) Now may I please see Susan? (*As she still hesitates*) She'll have to talk to someone sooner or later and it might as well be me.
Helen She's having her breakfast—she isn't exactly dressed.
Ian A dressing-gown?

Helen goes out R

Act II, Scene 2　　　　　　　　　　　　　　　　　　　　35

Ian (*to John*) Perhaps we can clear up a few points while we're waiting.
John (*indicating a chair to Ian*) Of course.
Ian (*sitting*) As you didn't know Mr Watson you wouldn't have visited him.
John That's right.
Ian So we're not likely to find any of your fingerprints in his bungalow.
John Fingerprints?

Helen enters with a dressing-gown, reacts, but crosses and exits

John I—I went there before he took over—so did Helen. We know the owners, Mr and Mrs Talbot.
Ian So any of your prints we find there must have been made before Mr Watson came?
John Could you prove otherwise?
Ian If one of yours happened to be on top of one of his.

Helen and Susan enter, L. Susan is doing up the dressing-gown. It has now dawned on her that Mr Watson's death could mean more than a little excitement in the avenue. She is a little over-casual, a little over-confident. Ian, having had experience, notices these signs, but Helen and John do not. Ian stands up as they enter

Helen (*to Ian*) I believe you've met my daughter Susan.
Ian For a moment, at the police ball. Good morning, Susan.
Susan Good morning. What did you want to know?
Ian Just when you arrived home last night.
Susan About midnight.
Ian With Michael of course?
Susan Of course.
Ian How long did it take you to say goodnight?
Susan I don't see that's——
Helen Susan!
Susan Only a minute or two. We'd had a row.
Ian In fact you were still having it.
Susan Maybe.
Helen I've told you before. The neighbours——
Susan —Are a pack of fuddy-duddies. (*To Ian*) What did they hear?
Ian Car doors slamming. Voices.
Susan Is that all?
Ian Why? Have we missed something?
Susan Nothing that concerns the police.
Helen Susan!
Susan It was personal.
Ian I'm sure it was. Did you see anything unusual on your way down the avenue?
Susan Such as that man Watson's body lying in the gutter? No I didn't.
John (*sharply*) Susan, don't talk like that!

Ian She doesn't mean anything, Mr Ferryman.
Susan (*strongly*) How do *you* know what I mean?
Ian (*quietly*) After more than twenty years in the force, frightened witnesses aren't new.
Susan Frightened! ⎫
Helen That's going too far. ⎬ (*Speaking together*)
John What on earth has Susan to be frightened of? ⎭

There is a sudden silence

Susan I'm sick of answering questions—and I'm tired of hanging round like this. I'm going to get dressed.

Before anyone can stop her Susan exits quickly, R. *At the same time the telephone begins to ring. They ignore it*

Helen (*following Susan*) Susan!

Helen exits R

Ian (*unperturbed*) Hadn't you better answer the phone?
John What?
Ian The telephone.

As John turns towards it Mrs Parks enters L, *having taken off her coat*

Mrs Parks Everybody deaf or something? (*Picking up the receiver*) Hello. . . . Yes.
John I'll take it.
Mrs Parks (*on the telephone*) Hang on. (*To John*) The surgery.
John Oh! (*going to door* R *and calling off*) The surgery for you, Helen. Will you take it on the extension? (*He crosses to Mrs Parks, takes the receiver from her, listens for a moment, then replaces the receiver. A dismissal*) All right, Mrs Parks.
Ian Just a minute.

Mrs Parks stops

I believe you used to work for Mr Watson.
Mrs Parks When he first came I did—now I don't.
Ian Why not?
Mrs Parks (*with difficulty*) Incomparibility of temper.
Ian I see. (*To John*) If you don't mind, Mr Ferryman, I'd like to take Mrs Parks over to Mr Watson's for a few minutes.
Mrs Parks What for? I ain't done nothing.
Ian I didn't say you had.
Mrs Parks So what do you want me to go there for?
Ian To see if anything's missing.
Mrs Parks Well that's different ain't it? I'll get me coat.

She exits, leaving the door open

Act II, Scene 2   37

Ian (*looking after her*) What do you know about her?
John Very little. My wife thinks she's a talkative, hard-working busybody.
Ian Just the kind of person who might uncover something you wanted to hide.

Mrs Parks enters

Mrs Parks (*struggling into her coat*) Well come on. What are we waiting for?
Ian (*indicating*) After you.

As Mrs Parks reaches the door, R, Helen enters

Helen (*almost bumping into Mrs Parks*) Where are you going?
Mrs Parks To do me duty.

Mrs Parks exits

Ian (*following*) I'm borrowing Mrs Parks for a few minutes. I hope you don't mind.
Helen Not at all.

Ian exits R

During the next scene John moves restlessly about. He is not really interested in Mrs Parks. He is simply trying to keep Helen from asking questions

Helen What's going on?
John The Inspector thinks that Mrs Parks might be able to tell them if anything's missing from the bungalow.
Helen For a minute I thought she'd been arrested.
John I'm not sure she shouldn't be.
Helen John . . .
John Are you certain she doesn't take things from here?
Helen Of course she takes things. A bar of soap—a few cigarettes . . .
John She's dishonest.
Helen They call it "perks". I know she does it. She knows I know. There are no questions asked and we get along fine. (*Intensely, almost hysterically*) For God's sake will you stop talking about Mrs Parks!

John stands motionless

Why did you tell the police you were in bed—and tell me you were out?

John says nothing

Please, John—I've got to know.

There is a knock on the back door

John (*seizing on the interruption*) Someone's at the door. I'd better see who it is.

John exits L, returning immediately, following Michael, who obviously has something on his mind. As they enter—

I'm afraid Susan isn't dressed yet.
Michael Good morning Mrs Ferryman. (*Backing uneasily*) Then perhaps I'd better call back.

Michael turns back to the door and comes face to face with John

John Just a minute, Michael. Were you drunk when you brought Susan home last night?
Michael (*evasively*) Why—why should you think that?
John The noise you made woke some of the neighbours.
Michael I'm sorry.
John Which doesn't answer my question. Were you drunk or not?
Michael (*after a moment*) I don't know.
John Oh, come on, Michael.
Michael I had two beers. No more than I've often had before. But I think the cold-cure tablets I'd been taking all day must have affected me.
John You mean—with the alcohol . . .
Michael (*to Helen*) That would explain it—wouldn't it, Mrs Ferryman? Afterwards everything became patchy. I remember some things—but not others.
Helen Have you any of the tablets left?
Michael Yes. (*He produces a small bottle and hands it to Helen*)

Helen goes to the window, shakes a couple of tablets on to her hand and examines them. Michael watches her anxiously

Helen How many had you taken?
Michael About—ten—I think.
Helen Wasn't that a bit foolish?
Michael Mother kept on nagging at me.
Helen The safe dose is six a day. Didn't your doctor warn you?
Michael I didn't get them from the doctor.
John Would they be enough—along with a few drinks—to account for Michael forgetting things?
Helen It's certainly possible—why? (*Realizing*) Oh, no!
John (*to Michael*) Did you come here down the avenue?
Michael (*puzzled*) No, I came across the park.
John Then you haven't heard what happened?
Michael Happened? Where?
John A hundred yards from here. The man we were talking about last night—that Mr Watson—was found dead. The police think he could have been knocked down by a car late last night.
Michael (*stunned; sinking into a chair*) Oh, my God.
Helen Have you looked at your car this morning?
Michael Why should I?
Helen Wouldn't there be marks—dents—scratches or something?
Michael There are plenty of those already.

John Still, you ought to go and look.
Michael After I've seen Susan.
Helen Why drag Susan into it?
Michael She was with me, wasn't she?
Helen Not on your way home. And she's already told the police she saw nothing on the way here.

Unnoticed Susan has entered, R, in time to hear the last speech. She is now fully dressed

Susan No. Michael. I didn't say that.
Michael Susan.
Helen You told Inspector Conway——
Susan That I didn't see anyone lying in the gutter. I didn't tell him I saw someone walking along the pavement.
Michael Someone you knew?
Susan (*to Michael*) My dear stepfather (*To Helen*) Your dear husband— (*to John*)—who told the police he was safely tucked up in bed. (*Pointing*) That hatch isn't soundproof.
John You deliberately listened!
Susan Did I know you were going to tell lies?
Helen What if John *was* out? Does he need your permission to go for a walk?
Susan He went out. (*Sarcastically*) You knew he'd gone out——
Helen I didn't know——(*She stops suddenly*)
Susan (*accusingly*) So you knew nothing about it—and you were still ready to lie to the police.
Helen I know that whatever John has done——
Michael Please!

They both stop

(*To John*) Mr Ferryman, what did you see last night?
John I—I . . .
Susan (*going to the telephone*) I'm going to contact the police.
Helen You'll do nothing of the kind!

Susan picks up the receiver

John I wouldn't advise you to make that call.
Susan I'm sure you wouldn't.
John For Michael's sake—not mine.

Michael tenses. Susan hesitates and looks at John

Because if I tell the police what I saw, Michael will spend the next few years of his life in prison.

There is a moment's tension. Susan replaces the receiver

Michael What did you see?

John Your car—going too fast—swinging from one side to the other—out of control.

Michael And—and Mr Watson?

John I found his body. At least one wheel of the car had gone right over him.

Susan Oh, no!

Michael (*horrified*) Oh, my God! (*He sits down, dazed and staring*) Then—then—there's nothing more to be said.

Susan (*kneeling by his side*) There's a lot more. You just can't sit back. What are you going to do?

Michael What *can* I do? I've got to go to the police. I've got to tell them I killed a man.

Susan Now you remember doing it?

Michael Of course I don't remember.

Susan So you're just going to repeat what my stepfather said.

Michael He was there. He saw what happened.

Susan Then let *him* go to the police.

Helen You're putting John in an impossible position.

Susan (*to Helen, strongly*) And what sort of a position is Michael in? Look Michael. If you'd known what you were doing. If you'd knocked him down and driven off in a panic—I wouldn't stop you confessing. But you didn't know—you were doped—you weren't responsible.

Michael Then who *was*?

The front doorbell rings violently. Helen goes quickly to the window and cautiously looks out, R

Helen (*to Michael*) It's your mother.

Michael I don't want to see her—not now. (*He rises quickly and goes to the door* L) I——

Susan But you can't just . . .

Michael (*in the doorway*) I need time to think.

He exits L

Susan hesitates undecided

Helen (*quietly*) Go with him, Susan.

Susan also exits L. *The front doorbell rings again*

Helen (*going to the door,* R) What are you going to say?

John shrugs helplessly

Helen exits, returning almost immediately preceded by Mrs Eastwood who almost bursts into the room. She is agitated and has obviously dressed in a hurry

Mary (*as she enters*) Isn't Michael here then?

Helen He—he's just left.

Act II, Scene 2

Mary Where was he going?
John To fetch his car I think.
Mary The police have confiscated it. For heaven's sake tell me what Michael's done.
Helen You mustn't upset yourself.
Mary (*with rising hysteria*) Something happened to Michael last night— I heard him when he came in. There was something wrong then. He drove in far too fast. He slammed the doors. He stumbled up stairs. I thought he was drunk. When I woke this morning the police were knocking on the door and Michael was gone. They said—there'd been an accident—that someone had been killed.
Helen Mr Watson.
Mary But what has Michael——
John His body was lying in the road.
Mary And Michael drove Susan home last night.
Helen Susan says nothing happened when she was with him.
Mary And afterwards?
Helen Michael can't remember.
Mary Then he *was* drunk.
Helen I don't think so. The whole trouble goes back to the tablets he'd been taking for a cold—far more than he should have done. Do you know where he got them?
Mary Oh, no—Oh God, no! I—I gave them to him. They were some Dr Lewis prescribed for me last year.
Helen Didn't he warn you about drinking or driving?
Mary He asked me if I drove a car. I told him I didn't—and he didn't say any more. I'd forgotten. (*Realizing Helen is staring at her*) I tell you I'd forgotten.
Helen (*looking away*) I'm sorry I didn't mean to——
Mary (*with rising hysteria*) No! You're quite right. It's all my fault. Oh, God—what have I done?
Helen You mustn't look at it like that. Michael took far too many tablets.
Mary He wouldn't have done if I hadn't kept getting on at him.
Helen He wasn't responsible.
Mary (*wildly*) But I am. I'm responsible for everything that's happened. I've got to find Michael—I've got to go to the police.
John I don't think——
Mary (*strongly*) What does it matter what you think—Michael's my son— and I—and I . . . (*She begins to sway*) I must—I must . . .
Helen (*urgently*) John!

John is just in time to catch Mary as she collapses. He places her on the settee. Helen kneels beside her and makes a quick examination

Mrs Parks puts her head through the door L

Mrs Parks Just thought I'd let you know I'm back. (*Seeing Mrs Eastwood and coming into room*) Here, what's the matter with Mrs Eastwood?

Helen Is the bed aired in the spare room?
Mrs Parks Ain't it always. For emergencies you said.
Helen This is an emergency.
Mrs Parks They why didn't you say so?
Helen Carry her, John, will you? (*To Mrs Parks*) Get some extra blankets then fix a hot-water bottle.
Mrs Parks No sooner said than done.
Helen (*she crosses to the telephone; to John*) I'll be with you as soon as I've had a word with Dr Lewis.

While Helen is dialling, John picks up Mary and carries her off R. *Mrs Parks holds the door open for him, then follows*

Mrs Parks (*as she exits*) You just put her on the bed then leave her to me. It ain't the first time by no means I've had to lay someone out.
Helen (*on the telephone*) This is Dr Ferryman. Could I speak to Dr Lewis? . . .

The front doorbell rings

(*Calling*) John! (*On the telephone*) Thank you. I'll hold on . . . (*The doorbell rings again. Calling*) John, will you answer the bell?
John (*off* R) O.K. I'm going.
Helen (*on the telephone*) Oh, good morning, Dr Lewis. This is Dr Ferryman. I'm speaking from my home—not the surgery. I have a patient of yours here—Mrs Mary Eastwood. . . . That's right. She collapsed after an emotional shock. . . . Everything points that way. . . . I couldn't send her home there's no-one to look after her, and if it's only for a few hours. . . . Of course, one-o-two Parkside Avenue, Orrell two-two-one-five. . . . You'll make all arrangements. . . . Thank you.

During this conversation John has ushered in Ian in time for him to hear Helen give Mary's name. He reacts and listens. John indicates a chair for him but he shakes his head. John moves towards Helen

John (*to Helen as she rings off*) Is there anything more I can do?
Helen Not at the moment, thanks. (*She crosses to the door* R)
Ian (*intercepting her*) What's wrong with Mary?
Helen She's had a shock. She collapsed. We've just put her to bed. Now if you'll excuse me.

She exits

Ian (*looking after her*) Mr Ferryman, perhaps you can tell me what's wrong. Your wife mentioned a shock.
John Your men went to collect Michael's car and gave her the impression that he was going to be arrested for a hit-and-run murder.
Ian My men wouldn't mention hit-and-run. We've never called it that.
John You said in this very room——

Act II, Scene 2   43

Ian —that we weren't sure how Mr Watson had died. You suggested hit-and-run and if Mary's got that impression she's got it from you.

Mrs Parks enters R, carrying a hot-water bottle and crosses to the door L

Mrs Parks (*stopping by Ian*) Here—did you manage to open that box I found?

John reacts slightly unnoticed by the others

Ian (*shortly*) Yes.
Mrs Parks What was in it? (*As Ian opens his mouth to say something*) You wouldn't have looked in the chimney but for me. I got a right to know.
Ian Private papers which are no concern of yours.
Mrs Parks (*sniffing*) Oh, well, that's different, ain't it?

She exits L

John (*casually*) I—I gather you found something then?
Ian (*shortly*) Yes.
John Some reason for Mr Watson being killed perhaps?
Ian (*blandly*) Reason? If he was killed accidentally how would there be a reason? Now do you know where Susan is? Or Michael?
John They went out together a little while ago.

The telephone rings. John answers it

Mrs Parks enters L and crosses with the now filled hot-water bottle. Ian drops back so that he is not immediately obvious to anyone entering L

John (*on the telephone*) Yes? . . . Oh, Dr Lewis. I know about it. Could I take a message? . . . The ambulance will call at twelve. I'll tell her. . . . Good-bye. (*He rings off*)

During the last few words of the call Susan has burst in L and almost run towards the door R. She is in a temper verging on tears. She ignores John and does not see Ian

John Susan!

Susan stops but does not turn round

Where's Michael?
Susan I don't know—and I don't care. I don't ever want to see him again. He's a silly—stupid—stubborn . . . (*Words fail her*)
Ian Pig-headed?
Susan Pig-headed! (*Realizing, facing Ian*) It's all your fault. If you hadn't brought him up like a policeman he might have had some sense.

Almost in tears she runs off R. As they stand looking after her, Michael appears in the doorway L. He is tense, almost to breaking-point

Michael Uncle Ian ...
Ian (*quietly*) Yes, Michael.
Michael I—I killed Mr Watson—I ran over him when I was driving home.
Ian I know. At least I know it was your car. I assumed you were driving it.
Michael Then—why haven't you ...?
Ian Because I knew—sooner or later—you'd come to me.

The stiffness goes out of Michael's body. He sways a little. Ian takes hold of his arm

Better sit down, son.

Ian helps Michael to a chair

(*To John, indicating drinks*) Mr Ferryman, would you ...?
Michael It was an accident. I didn't know——
Ian Not yet, son. Not to me. I'll take you down to the station and you can tell one of my men what happened. Sergeant Lever—you know him?
Michael Yes.

John hands Ian the drink and he in turn gives it to Michael

Ian You see I've learned from experience not to take statements from your own family—or people you love. You may be too involved to get them right.
Michael (*despondently*) Will you—tell my mother—what happened?
Ian I'll take care of everything. Now there's no need to look so gloomy. I'd be a fool to say you weren't in trouble. But you didn't even know the dead man—so no-one's going to call it murder.

Michael freezes with his glass in his hand ready to put it down

After all, you haven't any motive.

Michael lets the glass fall and as he looks quickly up at Ian with an expression of dawning horror—

the CURTAIN *falls*

ACT III

Scene 1

The Ferrymans' lounge. About 10.30 the same morning. The crockery, etc., has been cleared away and a vase of flowers is on the table. The serving-hatch is slightly open—so is the door R

As the Curtain *rises John ushers in Ian*

John Come in, Inspector.
Ian You sound as though you were expecting me.
John I thought you'd be back once you heard Michael's story.
Ian Yes it certainly makes a difference.

Susan bursts in R

Susan What have you done with Michael?
Ian Done?
Susan You took him away in a police car half an hour ago.
Ian He's simply making a statement and having his prints taken.
Susan Oh! Have you told him about his mother?
Ian I thought he'd enough to worry about. But if Mrs Ferryman thinks he's needed here I'll have him brought back and his statement can wait.

Helen has appeared in the doorway R, *in time to hear his last speech*

Helen That won't be necessary. Mrs Eastwood is still unconscious. Susan, would you go and sit with her.
Susan (*protesting*) But I want to know——
Helen (*over-riding*) Let me know if there's any change.
Susan But——
Helen Susan!
Susan Oh all right.

She flounces off R, *slamming the door*

Ian Just what *is* the matter?
Helen It's difficult to put into non-technical language—and after all I'm not a psychiatrist. Dr Lewis thinks this crisis has been building up for some time. What happened this morning was the last straw. She gave Michael those cold-cure tablets without warning him about possible side-effects, and now she feels completely responsible for everything that happened.

Ian Then this coma...

Helen A way of escape—a retreat from reality.

Ian Look, Doctor—I don't wish to question your knowledge—or experience—but isn't this explanation—a little...?

Helen (*quoting*) "When I went to see her she was clinging to the baby as if it was all she had left. And that's the way it's been ever since." Your words, Inspector. And what happens when you take away all that's left?

Ian How long is she likely to be like this?

Helen A day—a week—a month. Dr Lewis has arranged for her to go to Woodvale.

Ian That's a mental——

Helen She needs psychiatric treatment.

Ian Of course. Thank you for all you've done.

Helen I'm a doctor—and I'm fond of Michael. (*Rising and standing beside John*) But I'm sure you didn't come back just to enquire about Mrs Eastwood. What do you want to know?

Ian The truth about where you were—both of you—between ten-thirty and midnight.

Helen I was in bed.

Ian (*to John*) And you?

John Working in the study until nearly midnight. Then I went out for a stroll.

Ian Yes?

John (*after a moment*) On the way back I saw Michael's car coming down the avenue rather erratically. Then I found Mr Watson's body.

Ian Why didn't you report it?

John Report! Susan was very fond of her real father and has always resented my taking his place—I felt that if I reported Michael to the police the situation might become impossible—Susan might even leave home.

Ian And to stop that you were prepared to let Michael get away scot free?

John I was prepared to give him the chance to come forward of his own free will.

Ian And if he didn't?

John I—I don't know.

Ian (*to Helen*) So you were in bed—(*to John*)—and you were taking a stroll. Both of you were alone.

Helen What are you suggesting?

Ian You haven't an alibi between you.

Helen Why do we need an alibi? Mr Watson was killed in an accident.

Ian (*deliberately*) Mr Watson was killed by a blow on the head during a struggle in the lounge of his bungalow.

John and Helen react

We're not sure how his body got into the road—but when Michael ran over him—he was already dead.

The tension is broken by Mrs Parks bursting in L

Act III, Scene 1

Mrs Parks (*excitedly*) Murdered! I knew it. It was just the same when the old man next door pushed his wife downstairs. An accident they said. A bit of loose carpet they said. But I knew——

Ian (*loudly*) Mrs Parks!

Mrs Parks (*with injured innocence*) Well there's no need to shout.

Ian (*pointing to serving-hatch*) Have you been eavesdropping?

Mrs Parks (*on her dignity*) Eavesdropping 'as never been my 'abit. In the course of me duties I 'appened to be cleaning up near the 'atch. (*Back to normal*) Mind you, it stands to reason, don't it. If you go bobbing about in the bushes sooner or later someone's going to hit you with something.

Ian Are you talking about Mr Watson?

Mrs Parks Last night it was. Right outside that window. Gave me the fright of my life.

Helen Rubbish! She——

Ian (*to Helen, sharply*) Please! (*To Mrs Parks*) Why didn't you tell me this before?

Mrs Parks You didn't ask me. And they—(*indicating John and Helen*)—said to keep it quiet.

Ian Oh! they did? (*He looks suspiciously at Helen and John. To Mrs Parks*) What was he doing?

Mrs Parks Well he wasn't looking for birds' nests. Lurking, that's what he was doing and if you don't know what he was lurking for——

Ian All right, Mrs Parks.

Mrs Parks I was only trying to help.

Ian And I'm very grateful. Now would you go and sit with Mrs Eastwood so that Susan can come here. (*To Helen*) Would that be all right, Mrs Ferryman?

Helen As long as someone's with her.

Mrs Parks (*moving to the door*, R) Me name's Amelia Parks—(*in the doorway*)—not Florence Nightingale.

Mrs Parks exits R

Ian (*to John and Helen*) Well?

John This is a cul-de-sac. When the park gates are locked people climb over the wall into our garden to get out. No-one else saw Mr Watson—and you'd hardly call Mrs Parks a reliable witness.

Helen There's no doubt about how he died?

Ian None. And we know the time because a travelling-clock was broken in the struggle. It had stopped at eleven o'clock.

Helen You mean—for an hour—he was lying in the road?

Ian Most unlikely. The doctor thinks he could have lain unconscious in the bungalow for some time—then recovered sufficiently to stagger outside—presumably for help.

John Couldn't he use the phone?

Ian It was torn away. He got as far as the grass verge then collapsed again. There was blood . . .

John But he was lying in the gutter.

Ian The verge slopes quite steeply. Presumably he made a final effort and rolled down into the road. Or of course he could have been moved there by the murderer in the hope of making his death look like an accident.

During the last few speeches Helen has begun to sway a little. She sinks into a chair

Helen (*almost to herself*) Oh, God.
John (*going quickly to her*) Are you all right dear?
Helen It was just the thought of—of anyone—in the dark—trying to find help—then dying—alone.
John I'll get you a drink.
Helen No! No, thank you. It was silly of me. (*Pulling herself together*) What—what will happen to Michael?
Ian He'll be charged with driving while unfit to do so.
Helen Will he be sent to prison?
Ian I doubt it. A fine—endorsement—perhaps probation.
John And what are the charges against us?
Helen John!
John (*to Ian*) You talked about alibis. Do you think either of us capable of murder?
Ian Not in cold blood. But a blow in the heat of the moment. I think you're both capable of that.

Susan enters R

Or even you, Susan.
John So could a lot of people. Why pick on us?
Ian Because . . . you had a motive.
Susan (*puzzled*) A motive! What are you talking about?
Ian A photograph we found at Mr Watson's.
Helen (*shaken*) You couldn't. It's impossible!
Ian Why?
Helen (*covering up*) Well—well, why should any photograph you found there concern us?
Ian We found it tucked away inside a telephone directory.
John What makes you think——
Ian (*over-riding*) Let's not play games, Mr Ferryman. That kind of photograph isn't made for fun—it's made for blackmail. And Mr Watson *was* in your garden last night.
Helen You said—made?
Ian It's a fake.
Susan Michael and I—never did—(*perhaps a shade regretfully*)—anything.
Ian Is that bad?
Susan It is if he doesn't want to.
Helen Susan!
Susan Well he's certainly no wolf. I think he's too shy.
Ian Or perhaps he has too much respect for you.

Act III, Scene 1 49

John Doesn't that make your so-called motive a little thin?
Ian It depends on how many people believe what Susan says.
Susan Why do you keep talking about motives? What happened was an accident. Oh, Michael made threats about beating the living daylight out of Mr Watson——
Ian He did?
Susan (*hastily*) But that was just hot air—to impress me a little. We both knew that he'd have more sense than to do anything violent.
Helen (*warningly*) Susan!

Susan turns to look at her

Mr Watson wasn't killed accidentally. He was murdered.
Susan Murdered! Murdered! (*Turning to Ian*) And you think that Michael . . . ?
Ian He'd seen that photograph, hadn't he?
Susan What difference does that make? You've known him all his life—you should know better than anyone that Michael wouldn't kill anybody.
Ian Suppose he tried to take the photographs from Mr Watson—and there was a struggle?
Susan (*firmly*) Michael was with me at the dance.
Ian All the time?
Susan (*after a very slight hesitation*) Yes.

For a moment they stand facing each other, then Ian goes to the telephone

Ian With your permission. (*He dials*)
Susan What are you doing?
Ian Checking up.
Helen Michael's father was your best friend. He saved your life.
Ian Why do you think I'm here? Now I'm wondering whether it wouldn't have been better to leave it to someone else.
Susan Your job is more important than Michael. Is that what you mean?
Ian My job is to find the guilty and protect the innocent. If Michael is innocent he won't get hurt. If he's guilty at least I'll be on the spot to advise him. (*On the telephone*) Sergeant! . . . Conway here. Has Michael Eastwood left yet? . . . Then take him back a few hours. I want to know everything he did from eight o'clock onwards—Right! (*He rings off. To Susan*) And I hope his story agrees with yours.
Susan (*fuming, she glares at him then swings away*) We had a row. He was dancing all over the place. I thought he was drunk.
Helen That would be the tablets plus——
Susan How was I to know that?
Ian What happened after?
Susan I danced with some other boys—he got jealous. Then I couldn't find him.
Ian How long was he missing?
Susan (*firmly*) I don't know.
Ian When did you see him again?

Susan About an hour later.
Ian Did he say where he'd been?
Susan Sitting in the car.
Ian (*incredulously*) For an hour?
Susan I didn't cross-examine him.
Ian What time was it when he came back?
Susan I didn't look at my watch either.
Ian But you do remember when you left the dance?
Susan Just before midnight.
Ian You thought Michael was fit enough to drive?
Susan He said he felt a bit muzzy—but apart from that he seemed all right. It wasn't until he got into the car that he started to act up again.
Helen Had he taken any more tablets?
Susan He thought they might clear his head.
Ian But in spite of "acting up" as you call it you didn't try to stop him driving home after he'd dropped you?
Susan I was mad at him.
Ian He might have been killed.
Susan So I was wrong. I'm sorry. Anyway he hadn't far to go.
Ian And what was your stepfather doing when you saw him?
Susan He was—How did you know?
Ian Michael told us.
Susan He was walking on the opposite side of the road—about half-way between here and number thirty-seven.
Ian (*to John*) Then you must have seen Michael's car as you went out as well as when you came back.
John I didn't notice. My mind was still on the work I'd been doing. Cars aren't completely unknown in the avenue even at midnight.
Ian And bodies?
John What?
Ian If you walked up the avenue—on that side—you must have passed Mr Watson's body.
John I told you—I wasn't taking any notice. If I saw anything it didn't register.
Ian The car registered well enough on your way back.
John My mind was clearer. Besides I had the car in view for much longer.
Ian As long as it took Michael to drive out of the avenue?
John Yes!
Ian A short walk, wasn't it? To the main road and back.
John I was out for fresh air—not exercise.
Ian Perhaps to smoke a cigarette.
John Yes!
Ian What brand?
John Brand? Why these (*He takes a cigarette-case out of his pocket, opens it then closes it quickly. Susan is the only person who might be able to see inside the case*) Empty, I'm afraid. (*Turning to the divider*) Never mind there are some here. (*He picks up the box, opens it and holds it out to Ian*) Though I don't see why the police should be interested.

Act III, Scene 1 51

Ian (*taking one*) Didn't I tell you? We found one half-smoked along with Mr Watson's body.
Helen Aren't you clutching at straws?
Ian (*examining the cigarette*) Um?
Helen Dozens of cigarettes must be thrown away in this road every day. It could have been there for a long time.
Ian Not the one we're interested in. We found it caught up in Mr Watson's coat. It could only have got there while he was lying in the gutter. (*To John*) This your usual brand?
John I've smoked them for years.
Ian (*dropping the cigarette back into the box*) Then it couldn't have been you—but . . . (*Picking up the ash-tray*) With your permission I'll take these for the lab.

During the next few speeches Ian takes a plastic bag or envelope from his pocket and empties the contents of the ash-tray into it

John (*tensely*) The lab?
Ian Analysis of traces left on a cigarette by the person smoking it. They call it the saliva test.
Helen (*strongly*) John's already admitted that he saw the body.
Ian *After* the car had gone. (*To John*) That's right, isn't it?
John I've already told you.
Ian But this cigarette was dropped *before* the car came. The wheels which went over the body went over the cigarette as well. When we found it—it was squashed flat. (*Deliberately*) Whoever dropped it must have known Mr Watson was dead before the car touched him.

Helen gasps. Ian looks keenly at each in turn

Someone very much wanted us to think it was hit-and-run. I wonder who?

The tension is broken by the telephone ringing. Ian is the first to move

Ian That's probably for me (*On the telephone*) Yes? . . . Speaking. . . . Very interesting! . . . No, I'll come down myself (*He replaces the receiver then pauses a moment, thinking. To Helen*) Mrs Ferryman, I'd like you to come down to the station with me.
Helen The station!
John (*protesting*) That's ridiculous. Helen isn't going——
Susan (*protesting and overlapping*) My mother's done nothing. It's my stepfather——
Ian (*over-riding*) Please! (*There is a sudden silence. To Helen*) You can refuse if you wish. We have some articles which we think you might be able to identify.
John Things you found at Mr Watson's?
Ian I didn't say that.
Helen Why should you think . . .
Ian I'd rather not say anything more except that it would help our enquiries and save a lot of time.

Helen (*after a moment*) Very well. As long as you bring me straight back. I don't want to leave Mrs Eastwood too long.
Ian Of course.
Helen I'll get my coat.
John (*intercepting Helen as she goes to the door*, R) I don't think you should go on your own. I'll come with you.
Helen No! It's getting on for eleven and you have to deliver those papers to Mr Martin before half-past and you mustn't miss him. Take my car. The keys are on the hall table.

She squeezes his arm reassuringly and exits, R

Ian (*as he follows her*) By the way—I'd be grateful to both of you if you'd call in at the station some time today to have your fingerprints taken. (*In doorway, blandly*) For elimination purposes, of course.

He exits R

There is a moment's awkward silence

Susan (*suddenly but casually*) Will you give me a cigarette?
John (*automatically holding out his case*) Of course.
Susan (*strongly, accusingly*) So your case wasn't empty.

John tries to draw the case back but Susan snatches it

That's just what I thought.

John tries to get the case back from Susan but she eludes him. This action continues at the discretion of the producer. During it a cigarette is dropped, un-noticed by either, and a vase of flowers is knocked over

And these aren't the same kind as the ones in the box.
John Give them back.
Susan Not on your life. The police are going to be very interested in them—and in your late-night stroll.
John What do you mean?
Susan When I saw you, you weren't walking towards Mr Watson's—you were walking away—as if you'd just left. In fact if you'd gone on walking you'd have arrived home almost as soon as we did.
John That's why I turned back. I didn't want to interrupt your good-nights.
Susan I don't believe you. You'd no idea Michael was going to leave right away. We might have taken half an hour. So why *should* you come back so soon—so conveniently to see Michael's car drive away.
John I can explain.
Susan Oh, of course. You can explain everything. "I did it to protect Michael"—"I saw him run over Mr Watson but I didn't say anything because I wanted to act like your real father." (*Bitterly*) And I was beginning to believe you. Oh, you certainly fooled me.

Act III, Scene 1 53

John It wasn't like that at all.
Susan But it *was* your cigarette they found?
John Yes ...
Susan And you let Michael go on thinking he'd killed a man when you knew damn well he hadn't.
John I did what I thought was best.
Susan (*strongly*) To save your own skin!
John (*goaded*) To save Helen.
Susan (*stunned*) To save——! (*Recovering*) How low can you get?

For a moment they stand facing each other.

John (*quietly*) Whatever you think of *me*, Susan—you've got to believe what I'm telling you. If you go to the police with any of this—you'll put *your mother* in the dock—not me!

And as they stand motionless—

a quick CURTAIN

SCENE 2

The Ferryman's lounge. Almost 11.30 a.m. the same morning. The vase knocked over at the end of the last scene is still on its side. Both doors are open

The stage is empty. Sounds are heard off R *and Helen enters, followed by Ian. At the same time Mrs Parks enters* L. *Helen is obviously on edge*

Helen (*stopping as she sees Mrs Parks; sharply*) Have you left Mrs Eastwood alone?
Mrs Parks Only for a minute while——

Helen swings on her heel and exits R

Bit touchy, ain't she?
Ian Doctors expect their instructions to be carried out.
Mrs Parks All right, if you don't want the message.
Ian What message?
Mrs Parks From Sergeant Somebody or other. You got to phone the station as soon as you get here.
Ian (*irritably*) Then why didn't you say so?
Mrs Parks I just have.
Ian (*going to the telephone, dialling*) Why didn't you get Susan to sit with Mrs Eastwood?
Mrs Parks Because she went out with Mr Ferryman just after you.
Ian (*on the telephone*) Conway.... A print! Where?... Nowhere else?... No, leave it to me. Any joy with the other enquiries?... That's a turn

up for the books. Who've you sent?... Austin and Baker. Good. Let me know when they report. (*He rings off*)

Helen enters R

Helen (*to Mrs Parks*) You'd better get back.
Mrs Parks (*moving to the door* R) Okey-doke.
Ian (*who has just spotted the upset vase*) Just a minute.

Mrs Parks stops and turns

What happened after we left?
Mrs Parks Sitting out there I was, like I been told.
Ian You can hear just as much with the door open as you can through—(*indicating the hatch*)—there. How did this get knocked over?
Mrs Parks Must have been while they was having a barney.
Helen (*incredulously*) John and Susan?
Mrs Parks A real ding-donger.
Ian What about?
Mrs Parks "Cigarettes"—"Midnight walks"—"You let him think he had when you knew damn well he hadn't."
Ian And they left together straight afterwards?
Mrs Parks That's right.
Ian (*a dismissal*) Thank you very much.
Mrs Parks A pleasure, I'm sure.

She exits R

Ian (*to Helen*) You said that Mr Ferryman had to deliver some papers to a—Mr Martin. Is there any reason why he should take Susan?
Helen There's no reason why he shouldn't.
Ian Even after the row Mrs Parks overheard?
Helen Susan has a quick temper. It's soon up—but it's soon down.
Ian (*starting towards the telephone*) I think I'd better have a word with Mr Martin.
Helen You can't. He's on his way to New York.

As Ian turns back he spots the cigarette lying on the floor. He picks it up and looks at it

Ian Does Susan have a cigarette-case?
Helen No.
Ian Do you?
Helen It's in my bag.
Ian Then where did this come from?
Helen Is it the—kind—you found...?
Ian Yes!
Helen John's case was empty.
Ian Maybe Susan saw differently. And if Mr Ferryman lied about his cigarette-case she'd know that he let Michael be blamed for killing a man

Act III, Scene 2 55

who was already dead. (*Quoting*) "You let him think he had when you knew damn well he hadn't."
Helen Then she'd hardly drive away with him.
Ian Maybe she had no choice.

Helen registers apprehension, followed by disbelief

I'd like another word with Mrs Parks.
Helen Very well! (*She opens the door* R *and calls off*) Mrs Parks! (*To Ian*) You're not suggesting that John—kidnapped Susan?
Ian She's the only person who could give evidence against him.

Mrs Parks enters R

Mrs Parks I wish some people would make up their minds.
Ian When Susan left with Mr Ferryman did you see her get into the car?
Mrs Parks How could I? It was in the garridge.
Ian You've no idea how she got there?
Mrs Parks Well she didn't drop in through the roof. These days they're making 'em with doors.
Ian (*sharply; a dismissal*) All right, Mrs Parks.
Mrs Parks Nothing else you'd like to know?
Ian Quite.
Mrs Parks You wouldn't like me to hang on just in case.
Ian (*firmly*) No, thank you!
Mrs Parks Because all this walking ain't doing me varicus veins no good.

She exits R

Ian (*going to the telephone*) What kind of car is it?
Helen (*tensely*) What are you going to do?
Ian Have it picked up.
Helen No!
Ian Susan could be in danger.
Helen Not from John. Susan would only be a threat to him if he'd killed Simon. And I know he didn't.
Ian (*after a pause*) How do you know?
Helen (*hedging*) He—he had no reason.
Ian If he'd found out that your first husband was still alive he had every reason.
Helen If! If! If!
Ian Mr Watson didn't need that diary and snapshot to prove his identity to someone who knew him. He wanted them to convince someone who'd never seen him before.
Helen Are those the only papers you found?
Ian No. There were others.
Helen And what are you doing about them?

Ian Everything we can. I've a dozen men out—searching—checking—interviewing—watching and waiting for someone to move.
Helen But until someone does you're assuming that John is the murderer.
Ian I'm following the evidence.
Helen Fingerprints—saliva tests—alibis. Evidence is more than that. It's knowing the way people act and feel. And I know John wouldn't kill anybody.
Ian Would *you*?
Helen (*taken aback*) Me?
Ian You'd exactly the same motive—the same means—the same opportunity. And you've consistently lied about your movements—Did Mr Ferryman see you go into the bungalow?
Helen He couldn't have done. He was working in the study—— (*She stops suddenly, hand to mouth, eyes wide, staring at Ian*)

John enters R. *Helen almost runs to him*

(*Near to tears*) Oh, John. Thank God you've come.
John (*puzzled; putting his arms around her*) What on earth's the matter? (*To Ian*) Are you responsible for this?
Ian Where's Susan?
John You should know. (*To Helen*) Come and sit down.

John takes her to the settee and sits beside her

Helen The Inspector thinks you've kidnapped Susan to stop her giving evidence.
John And you believed him?
Helen Of course not.
Ian I want to know where Susan is.
John (*after a moment*) I dropped her at the police station half-an-hour ago.

Ian goes to the telephone

Ian (*dialling*) You know that Susan's evidence could put you in a very difficult position.
John *I* know it—but how do you if you haven't seen her?
Ian Something overheard by Mrs Parks. (*Holding out the cigarette*) And this cigarette. You admit it's yours?
John (*after a moment*) No point in denying it. I ran short yesterday and filled my case up at the office.
Ian (*on the telephone*) Conway.... Has a young lady called at the station within the last hour? Susan Lovat—seventeen— (*add a short description*). I'll hold on.

During this speech John has rejoined Helen on the settee

Helen You took Susan to the police knowing what she was going to say?
John (*rather ruefully*) I hadn't much choice. She believed I'd put Michael in danger to protect myself. If I'd tried to stop her she'd have taken it as proof that she was right. If I helped her—at least there was a chance she'd change her mind.

Act III, Scene 2   57

Ian (*on the telephone*) Thank you. (*He rings off*) No young lady answering to Susan's description has called at the station at any time today.
John Then she did change her mind.
Ian (*moving to* L *of the settee*) Or maybe you took her somewhere else?
John I dropped her on the Odeon corner.
Ian You said the station.
John It was the nearest I could get. Look—if I'd made sure Susan wouldn't be giving evidence—would I have admitted that she'd any to give?

Susan slips past the window from R *to* L. *She is visible only to Ian and the audience*

Ian pauses a moment but shows no other reaction

Ian (*moving round the back of the settee*) All right. For a moment I'll accept your story. (*Facing John*) Now Mr Watson was blackmailing you.

John opens his mouth to speak but Ian over-rides

We found records in the bungalow. And last night you arranged to meet him and buy him off but you found the price too high.
John (*strongly*) No!
Ian No—you didn't meet him? Or no—the price was right?
John I met him—but I didn't pay him anything.

At an appropriate moment the serving-hatch opens slightly

Ian What time was that?
John Nine o'clock.
Ian And you left him?
John About a quarter of an hour later.
Ian And went back at eleven.
John (*strongly*) It was half-past eleven when I left here and Mr Watson was already dead.
Ian But Susan saw you at midnight.
John That was after I'd been in the bungalow.
Ian To remove any incriminating evidence. And you wrecked the place looking for it.
John The place was already wrecked.
Ian Then exactly what did you do?
John —There was a candlestick—I picked it up before I realized there was blood on it.
Ian You wiped it clean?
John I was afraid you'd find fingerprints.
Ian Then?
John I left. I lit a cigarette. I was worried. I hadn't found anything—and then——
Ian It struck you he might have the evidence on him.
John I heard a car coming down the avenue. When it passed me I realized it was Susan and Michael. I went back to search the body. I had to move

it to get at some of the pockets. It began to roll down the slope—I couldn't stop it.

Ian When did you realize you'd dropped your cigarette?

John I never gave it a thought.

Ian You didn't really think we'd call Mr Watson's death accidental?

John There was always a chance. Someone breaks in—he's interrupted—there's a struggle—he runs out into the road——

Ian —and Mr Watson follows and is knocked over by a passing car. It's about as plausible as your story about the candlestick. And I don't believe that one either.

John I've told you the truth.

Ian About what you did—but not about why.

Helen How can you possibly know that?

Ian By asking myself one question. Would your husband really let Michael go to prison to protect an *unknown* burglar? (*To John*) Just how did you find out that Mrs Ferryman had also called on Mr Watson last night?

John Because I—— (*He stops abruptly*) I don't know what you're talking about.

Helen (*quietly*) It's no use, dear. I gave myself away. (*Looking straight into his eyes*) But I swear I didn't kill him. You must believe that.

John (*after a moment. Without moving*) I noticed your mac was wet—and inside the bungalow—the perfume you were using—I couldn't mistake that.

Helen You cleaned the candlestick because you thought——

John I only knew you'd been there—and that the police mustn't find out.

Helen Oh, my dear.

For a moment John holds her close

Ian (*coughing*) Mrs Ferryman!

Helen (*breaking away*) I'm sorry.

Ian When did you find out that your first husband was still alive?

Helen Last night—I caught a glimpse of him through the window.

Ian And when you went to the bungalow—were there any signs of other visitors?

Helen No.

Ian You met no one on the way?

Helen I *did* see a woman driving a car. I thought she was going to stop—but when she saw me she drove on.

Ian What time was that?

Helen A little after half-past ten.

Ian What happened when you met your first husband?

Helen I gave him an open cheque for two thousand pounds and a covering letter for the bank. He gave me the photographs and negatives and I burned them.

Ian We found the ashes but not the cheque.

Helen He put it in his inside pocket. I saw him.

Ian (*to John*) Did *you* find it, Mr Ferryman?

Act III, Scene 2

John No!

Ian I see. (*To Helen*) How were you going to make him stay officially dead?

Helen I threatened to let the police have evidence that would convict him of dope peddling.

Ian Evidence you hadn't given us before because he was your husband?

Helen (*strongly*) Because he was Susan's father.

John I can't understand why he ever came back.

Helen Money! Revenge! To hurt me through Susan.

John And that's why he—made—those photographs? He would actually use his own daughter—

Helen To get what he wanted Simon would use anybody.

Ian But surely to carry out your threat you would have had to tell Susan the truth about her father.

Helen I'm beginning to realize that hiding the truth from Susan was the biggest mistake I ever made.

Ian I'm glad you said that. (*He opens the door* L *and speaks off*) Have you heard enough?

Helen and John stand motionless, staring, as Susan slowly appears in the doorway. Her face is white and strained

Susan Mother—I—I——

Breaking down, she almost runs to Helen who takes her in her arms

Helen Oh, my dear.

After a moment Susan breaks away striving for control. She goes slowly to John

Susan (*flatly*) I—I seem to have been—making a fool of myself—for quite a long time.

Crying, Susan runs out R

Helen (*hurrying after her, calling*) Susan! Susan!

Helen exits R

John (*to Ian accusingly*) You knew Susan was in there.

Ian I saw her coming across the garden.

John (*strongly*) You deliberately let her find out about her father like that.

Ian (*equally strongly*) Can you think of an easy way of doing it? (*The telephone rings. He snatches up the receiver. Still loudly*) Yes! . . . (*Normally*) I'm sorry. Go ahead. . . . They have? Good! . . . No! No, we'll try an experiment. Tell Austin to bring her here before he goes to the station. . . . One hundred and two Parkside Avenue. I'ts a cul-de-sac south of the park.

He replaces the receiver as Michael enters, L

John (*surprised*) Michael! Were you in there with Susan?
Michael (*vaguely*) What?—Susan?—No, I've just come from home. I was looking for Mother.
John Your mother's in bed here. She—she's not very well. Helen's looking after her.
Michael Why wasn't I told?
Ian I thought you had enough to worry about.
Michael You had no right——
Ian Dr Ferryman assured me that there was nothing you could do.

Michael stares at him for a moment, then swings on his heel and moves towards the door, R

Ian (*sharply*) Just a minute, Michael.
Michael (*not stopping*) I'm going to see Mother.
Ian (*cutting in between Michael and the door*) Not until you've answered a few questions.
Michael (*white-faced*) Let me pass. I want to talk to her.
John You can't. She's asleep.
Ian Instead perhaps you'll talk to me—(*meaningly*)—about last night. (*To John*) A few moments alone if you don't mind, Mr Ferryman.
John (*after a moment*) I'll be in the study.

John exits R

Ian (*quietly*) Won't you tell me just what you did?
Michael (*rather uncertainly*) You can't prove that I did anything.
Ian We found your fingerprints on Mr Watson's door—by the bell-push.

Michael sinks slowly on to the settee

What time did you call there?
Michael (*flatly*) I don't know.
Ian Michael!
Michael (*with more feeling*) I tell you I don't know. I'd had a row with Susan—I sat in the car for a long time feeling pretty grim. Everything seemed to have gone wrong—and it all went back to that man Watson.
Ian So you decided to go and tackle him.
Michael I rang the bell—but no-one answered. By that time I'd cooled off—and realized I was only making a fool of myself. So I drove back.
Ian What time did you get back to the dance?
Michael It was after eleven. In any case—what does it matter. Mr Watson wasn't killed as early as that—he was killed at midnight—when I ran over him.

After a moment

Ian So Sergeant Lever didn't tell you?
Michael (*suddenly apprehensive*) Tell me—what?
Ian That Watson died at half-past eleven from a wound inflicted at least half an hour earlier.

Michael And when I ran over him?
Ian He was already dead.
Michael (*with sudden realization*) No! Oh, God—no! (*Standing up*) I'm not answering any more questions—I'm going to see Mother.
Ian It's no use, Michael——

But Michael has swung on his heel and exited quickly, R. *Ian shakes his head, mutters "Damn and blast" then follows him as far as the door*

(*Calling off*) Mr Ferryman!
John (*off*) Yes, Inspector.
Ian Would you ask Mrs Ferryman if she can spare a few minutes. It *is* important.
John (*off*) All right, Inspector.

Ian moves up centre and takes a walkie-talkie out of his pocket and is about to talk into it when Mrs Parks enters R *and crosses to him*

Mrs Parks Here! That's a walkie-talkie ain't it?
Ian (*sharply*) What are you doing here?
Mrs Parks Going home.
Ian What about Mrs Eastwood?
Mrs Parks There's three of them out there. Enough to run a hospital. Besides, me time's up and Joe'll be waiting for his dinner.
Ian Don't let me detain you.
Mrs Parks Of course, if you've any more questions . . .
Ian (*quickly*) Not on your——I mean—No, thank you, Mrs Parks.
Mrs Parks Well, I suppose you know what you're doing. (*Sniffing*) Though if you ask me you need all the help you can get. Take them Starsky and Hutch—they don't need no walkie-talkie. Got a built-in set as you might say.
Ian (*opening the door* R; *firmly*) Thank you, Mrs Parks.
Mrs Parks Like that is it? Well I'm sure I'm not one to stay where I'm not wanted. (*In the doorway*) But the next time anyone says our police are wonderful—I'll tell 'em a thing or two!

Mrs Parks "sails out"

Ian (*into the walkie-talkie*) Oscar Delta Five. . . . Give me talk through to Alpha Charlie One Zero, Sergeant Austin. (*After a pause*) Oscar Delta Five calling Austin. Come in Austin (*He switches over*)

After a moment Sergeant Austin's voice is heard over the walkie-talkie

Austin's Voice Austin here. Over.

Ian switches back

Ian Report your last position. Over. (*He switches over*)

Austin's Voice Elton Road, approaching junction with Parkside Avenue. Over.

Ian switches back

Ian Good. I'll expect you any minute. Thank you. Talk through completed. Over and out.

As Ian puts the set away Helen enters R

Helen I haven't much time.
Ian This won't take long. I'm expecting an important witness here in half-a-minute. I'd like you to be present.
Helen Why?
Ian I'd rather not say.
Helen Isn't this a bit cloak and dagger?
Ian Cloak and dagger sometimes works.

There is a sound of a car stopping outside. Ian goes quickly to the window and looks off, R

With your permission I'll let them in.

Ian exits, returning almost immediately ushering in Rita Davies, but a very different Rita from the young lady we saw earlier in the play. The glamour has gone and the guttersnipe is showing through. Her blonde hair is covered by a long, dark-coloured, natural-looking wig. Her manner of speaking is coarser. Her make-up is different. If the audience at first fail to recognize her, so much the better. She is carrying a handbag. While this is going on Helen backs rather tensely left and watches

Ian (*as he enters he speaks into hall*) You wait there, Austin. We can manage.

Ian is followed in by Policewoman Baker, who closes the door and stands with her back to it

Rita (*looking around*) What the hell is this? A tour of the stately homes?
Ian You'll find out. (*To Baker*) Did she give you any trouble?
Baker Not really, sir. (*She holds out a passport and a small key on a ring*) These might interest you, sir. She was using them to try and get hold of the safe-deposit box.
Rita (*trying to snatch them*) Damn you! They're mine.
Ian (*evading her and motioning Baker to watch her. Looking at the passport*) Well, well—Mr and Mrs.
Rita You've got no right——
Ian (*closing the passport; swinging the key round*) A stupid thing to do, wasn't it—trying to get hold of that box without the receipt. But when you couldn't find it I suppose you had to take a chance. You certainly wrecked the place looking for it.

Act III, Scene 2 63

Rita I don't know what you're talking about.
Ian And you didn't clean up very well. Prints all over the study—in the bedroom . . .
Rita So an old man wanted a bit of fun.
Ian You don't need a passport for that kind of fun. You helped him in his racket, didn't you? You carried the drugs to the pushers.
Rita I never touched the stuff.
Helen (*realizing*) Why—why you're just one of Simon's floosies.
Rita (*swinging on her; to Ian*) Who's she? (*To Helen*) And who the hell are you calling a floosie?
Ian (*to Helen*) Do you recognize this—er—lady?
Helen (*doubtfully*) It—could be . . . (*Shaking her head*) No—no. I'm sorry.
Ian Perhaps this will help.

Moving quickly Ian whips off Rita's wig

Rita (*snatching the wig back and stuffing it into her pocket*) Take your hands off me!
Helen That—that's the woman I saw last night driving the car.
Rita You're a liar. I was nowhere near the place.
Ian What place?
Rita Wherever she was.
Helen You drove past the bungalow about half-past ten.
Rita What if I did? Is this a private road or something? Did you see me stop? Did you see me go in?
Helen No—no. I . . .
Ian We found footprints outside the french windows.
Helen Of course! You didn't drive away—you stood outside the window and listened to everything I said.
Rita I tell you I wasn't even there. (*To Ian*) Look, why should I kill him? I was doing all right, wasn't I. He was going to marry me—he was taking me to Spain——
Helen He wasn't taking you anywhere—and you knew it. And he couldn't marry you because he was already married to me. You realized he'd just been fooling you—and when I'd gone you had a show-down. (*Strongly*) There was a fight and you killed him!
Rita (*almost shouting*) What the hell are you talking about. All right, I drove past the bungalow—and I saw you going in so I went away—I drove round a bit—I tried to phone him but I couldn't get through. When I got back soon after eleven o'clock you'd gone—and he was dead.
Ian Are you sure?
Rita I didn't do a post-mortem but he looked pretty dead to me. (*With rising hysteria*) And it wasn't me who killed him—it was you!

Suddenly Rita tries to attack Helen but Baker grabs her. There is a struggle during which Rita drops her bag which bursts open

(*Screaming*) He meant trouble for you—so you killed him!

With a final effort before being dragged back Rita spits in Helen's face

John bursts in R

John What the devil's going on? (*Going to Helen*) Are you hurt?
Helen No! No! . . .
John (*turning to Ian*) My God, Inspector . . . !
Helen Please, John—she didn't touch me—I'm all right.

Meanwhile Ian has calmly picked up Rita's handbag and taken out four bundles of five-pound notes

Ian Two thousand pounds, I think. And I imagine the cashier will remember who cashed the cheque.
Rita It's mine. I got a right——
Ian What right?
Rita I helped him, didn't I?
Ian In blackmail? Dope peddling?
Rita (*struggling in Baker's grip*) Damn you to hell!
Ian (*to Baker, putting the money back in the handbag*) Charge her with stealing this lot. That'll do to hold her.

Baker steers Rita towards the door L. *As she passes Ian Rita makes an effort to get at him*

Rita You bastard! I'll——

But Baker propels her out of the room and the sounds of their departure fade away. Ian closes the door

Helen Do you think she killed him?
Ian I doubt it.
John She stole the money.
Ian She also accused Mrs Ferryman of murder—and meant it.
John That's ridiculous.
Ian You didn't think so when you wiped the candlestick.
Helen (*despondently*) So we're back to where we started.
Ian Not quite. After all she *did* find the cheque. If either of you had killed Mr Watson there wouldn't have been any cheque there for her to find. You'd have destroyed it.

The door R *opens quietly and Michael can be seen in the hall listening, unnoticed*

Ian What time did you leave Mr Watson?
Helen About a quarter to eleven.
Ian And Rita arrived about five past. When you left he was alive. When Rita got there he was apparently dead. In between there was someone else . . .
Michael (*coming into the room*) It was me.

Act III, Scene 2

They all turn to face him. Helen and John are about to protest but Ian quietens them with a gesture. Michael moves slowly downstage

I lied before about what happened. When no-one answered the bell I went round to the back. I thought I'd see if he had a dark-room—or more photographs. I got in through the french windows. Someone came at me—he got his hands round my throat—I grabbed hold of something —I don't know what it was—I just went on hitting and hitting . . . (*He collapses on to the settee, his head in his hands*)

Ian (*standing behind him quietly*) Then you drove back to the dance as if nothing had happened.
Helen For God's sake, Inspector.

Once again he silences her with a gesture

Ian You were in the bungalow—in the dark. You had to find your way about—you touched things—the furniture—a door . . .
Michael I suppose I must have done.
Ian Then why didn't you leave any prints?
Michael (*almost desperately*) I—I had my gloves on.
Ian And you took them off just to ring the bell.
Michael (*trapped*) I——I——
Ian Who are you covering up for, son? Susan? Your mother?

Michael suddenly stiffens

Of course—your mother . . .
Michael No! No!
Ian When you drove up to Mr Watson's you saw your mother in the avenue. But as long as you thought he'd been killed at midnight it wasn't important. It was only when you found out when he really died that you realized she must have killed him.
Michael (*standing facing Ian; hysterically*) Don't *say* that. Mother's ill— I tell you she's ill . . .!
Ian (*quietly, after a moment*) I know, son. But what I said is true, isn't it?

Michael tries to say something, but can't, and sinks down on to the settee, his head in his hands

Susan enters R

Susan (*urgently as she enters*) Mother, Mrs Eastwood insists on getting up. I had to find her a dressing-gown. (*Seeing Michael*) Michael! (*She runs across and kneels beside him*) Michael, what's the matter?

Unable to speak Michael takes hold of her hands

(*To Ian accusingly*) What have you done to him?
Ian Only what I had to do.

The front doorbell rings. John goes quickly to the window and looks out

John It's the ambulance.

Helen Ask them to back into the driveway will you, John.

John nods and exits quickly R

(*To Susan*) Susan, go back to Mrs Eastwood.

She stops as Mary enters. She is wearing a dressing-gown and slippers, neither being a good fit. Her hair is untidy—her face pale and drawn. At first her manner is calm and her voice quiet, only her hands betraying her emotion. As the scene progresses she works up almost to hysteria. She crosses slowly to Ian

Mary I asked Michael to tell you what happened.

Ian He didn't have to, Mary.

Mary (*at first to Ian, then to all*) You see, I couldn't pay him the money he wanted for that—that photograph. So I went back again later to try and take it—(*with rising hysteria*)—but he caught me—I'd swore I'd go to the police. He got hold of me—(*rubbing her wrists*)—and I struggled to get away—I was frightened. There was a candlestick—I had to hit him to stop him. What else could I do?

Helen (*going to Mary*) You mustn't think about it.

Mary I didn't *mean* to kill him.

Ian In heaven's name why didn't you come to me to begin with?

Mary I was afraid. That photograph—Susan—Michael's career. I thought you'd be angry.

Ian (*gently*) Mary dear—after all these years you should have known me better than that. (*Putting his arm around her shoulders*) Now your doctor thinks you need a rest and someone to look after you so he's arranged for you to go to hospital for a while. The ambulance is here and Michael will go with you.

Susan (*going to Mary*) May I come too?

For a moment Susan and Mary look into each other's eyes then Mary reaches out and presses Susan's arm

Mary Thank you.

Helen I'll bring up everything you need.

John enters L

John (*in the doorway*) They're ready.

Helen (*to John*) Would you and Susan take Mrs Eastwood? I'd like a word with Michael.

John Sure.

John takes Mary's arm and they move towards the door

Mary (*in the doorway, turning*) Ian—you'll look after Michael?

Ian Haven't I always?

Mary smiles a little, nods and exits L, *assisted by John. Susan follows but stops before reaching the door*

Susan Whatever happens, Michael—to you—or your mother—I'm on your side.

She exits L

Helen (*sitting down by Michael*) Don't worry—your mother will get the best possible treatment. (*To Ian*) Isn't that so, Inspector?
Ian She'll have the best advice and care we can get.
Michael How long will it be—before . . . ?
Helen Six months—perhaps a year.
Michael And afterwards?
Helen She'll need a home—love—understanding. A lot will depend on you—and perhaps on Susan.
Michael Susan? No, I couldn't ask her . . .
Helen I imagine Susan will decide that for herself. (*Practically*) Are you ready?

Michael stands up. As he moves towards the door he comes face to face with Ian

Ian I'm sorry, son. In this job you can't dodge the unpleasant things—however much you want to. You're father would have understood.
Michael Someday I think I'll understand too.
Ian That's all I want.

A look of understanding passes between them. Then Ian steps back and Michael exits L. *As he does so John enters* L

John So it's all over.
Ian (*moving towards the door*, R) As far as we are concerned. Now it's up to the lawyers.
John Lawyers? You mean the defence?
Ian I mean that a few years ago they decided that Simon Lovat had been burned to death in a car crash. They're going to have to do some hard thinking before they can charge Mary with *killing a dead man.*

As Ian exits R *and John and Helen stand looking after him—*

the CURTAIN *falls*

FURNITURE AND PROPERTY LIST

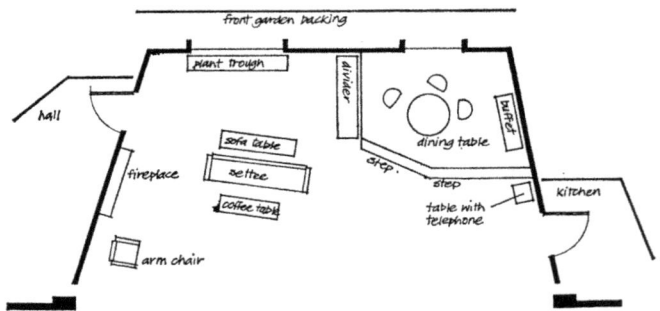

ACT I

On stage: Armchair
Plant trough
Sofa table
Coffee-table
Sofa
Room-divider. *On it:* glasses and drinks, cigarette box
Dining-table. *On it:* papers
Three chairs
Buffet
Table. *On it:* telephone, directories

Other dressing as desired

Off stage: Coffee-tray. *On it:* coffee things for three **(Helen)**
Suitcase **(Susan)**

Personal: **Michael:** suitcase, envelope containing photograph
Mrs Eastwood: envelope containing photograph

Driven to Murder 69

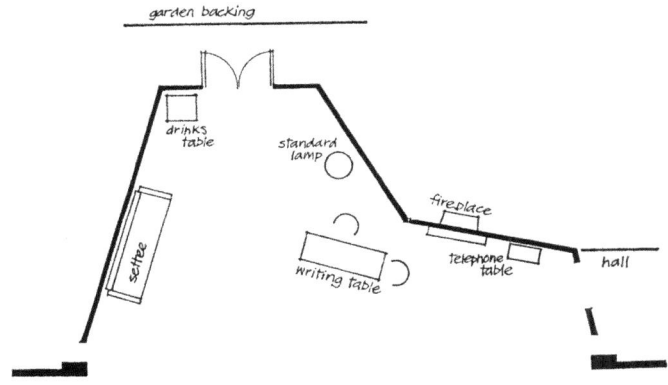

ACT II

Scene 1

On stage: Settee
Drinks table. *On it:* glasses and bottles
Standard lamp
Writing-table. *On it:* travelling-alarm-clock, magnifying-glass, candlesticks
Two chairs
Table. *On it:* telephone, directories
Electric fire
Waste-paper bin

Other dressing as desired

Set: In desk drawer: pair of white cotton gloves, 4 small white packets sealed with wax, handbag identical to **Rita's**, passport.
Metal box, containing photograph, diary, envelope containing 35mm negative, in chimney

Personal: **Rita:** handbag
John: envelope
Mary: screwdriver, torch
Helen: cheque and envelope, cigarette lighter
Watson: two airplane tickets

ACT II

Scene 2

Set: Breakfast things on table for three, including cereals

Off stage: Coffee-pot **(Helen)**
Toast-rack **(Mrs Parks)**
Tray **(Mrs Parks)**
Dressing-gown **(Helen)**
Hot-water bottle **(Mrs Parks)**

Personal: **John:** cigarette-case, matches
Michael: bottle of tablets

ACT III

Scene 1

Strike: Breakfast things

Set: Vase of flowers on dining-table

Personal: **John:** cigarette-case
Ian: plastic bag

ACT III

Scene 2

Personal: **Ian:** walkie-talkie radio
Rita: handbag containing four bundles of £5 notes
Baker: passport, key on ring

LIGHTING PLOT

Property fittings required: nil except for inset scene requiring standard lamp
An open-plan lounge with living-room inset

ACT I

To open: Lights in room on. Electric fire glows. Darkness outside
No cues

ACT II, SCENE 1

To open: Lights on. Electric fire on

Cue 1	**Mr Watson** switches off lights *Lights off, fire remains on. Fade to Black-out*	(Page 25)
Cue 2	Clock chimes the quarter *Firelight faded in. Moonlight outside window*	(Page 26)
Cue 3	**Intruder** takes refuge behind curtains *Light goes on in hall, followed by standard lamp*	(Page 26)
Cue 4	**Mr Watson** switches lamp off *Snap off lamp. Moonlight.*	(Page 30)
Cue 5	**Mr Watson** drags curtains open *Black-out*	(Page 30)

ACT II, SCENE 2

To open: Bright sunshine
No cues

ACT III, SCENE 1

To open: Bright sunlight
No cues

ACT III, SCENE 2

To open: Sunshine
No cues

EFFECTS PLOT

ACT I

Cue 1	**Helen** pours coffee *Telephone rings*	(Page 1)
Cue 2	**John:** "And you?" *Kettle whistles*	(Page 11)
Cue 3	**John:** ". . . just a crank after all." *Front doorbell rings*	(Page 12)
Cue 4	**Helen:** "You know we can't." *Front doorbell rings*	(Page 12)
Cue 5	**Helen:** ". . . what will he do?" *Front doorbell rings*	(Page 15)
Cue 6	**Ian:** ". . . must be going." *Telephone rings*	(Page 17)

ACT II, SCENE 1

Cue 7	**Mr Watson** puts on his jacket *Telephone rings*	(Page 20)
Cue 8	**Mr Watson** removes metal box from chimney *Doorbell rings once; then again*	(Page 22)
Cue 9	**Mr Watson** puts box inside chimney *Telephone rings*	(Page 25)
Cue 10	During Black-out *Clock chimes the quarter*	(Page 26)
Cue 11	**Mary** exits *Clock chimes the half-hour*	(Page 27)
Cue 12	**Mr Watson** sips drink *Front doorbell rings once; then again*	(Page 27)

ACT II, SCENE 2

Cue 13	**Susan:** ". . . talk about it?" *Doorbell rings*	(Page 33)
Cue 14	**Susan** exits *Doorbell rings again*	(Page 33)

Cue 15	**Susan** exits *Telephone rings*	(Page 36)
Cue 16	**Michael:** "Then who *was*?" *Doorbell rings violently*	(Page 40)
Cue 17	**Susan** exits *Doorbell rings again*	(Page 40)
Cue 18	**Helen:** ". . . speak to Dr Lewis? . . ." *Front doorbell rings*	(Page 42)
Cue 19	**John:** ". . . a little while ago." *Telephone rings*	(Page 43)

ACT III, SCENE 1

| Cue 20 | **Ian:** "I wonder who?"
Telephone rings | (Page 51) |

ACT III, SCENE 2

Cue 21	**Ian:** ". . . easy way of doing it?" *Telephone rings*	(Page 59)
Cue 22	**Ian:** "Come in Austin." *Talk-back through walkie-talkie radio*	(Page 61)
Cue 23	**Ian:** ". . . dagger sometimes works." *Car draws up*	(Page 62)
Cue 24	**Ian:** ". . . what I had to do." *Doorbell rings*	(Page 65)

MADE AND PRINTED IN GREAT BRITAIN BY
LATIMER TREND & COMPANY LTD PLYMOUTH
MADE IN ENGLAND

www.ingramcontent.com/pod-product-compliance
Ingram Content Group UK Ltd.
Pitfield, Milton Keynes, MK11 3LW, UK
UKHW021840210426
5322IPUK00022B/393